TAKING MEN ALIVE

ALIVE

EVANGELISM ON THE FRONT LINES

JIM WILSON

canonpress
Moscow, Idaho

Published by Canon Press, P.O. Box 8729, Moscow, ID 83843
800.488.2034 | www.canonpress.com

Jim Wilson, *Taking Men Alive: Evangelism on the Front Lines*
Copyright © 2014 by James I. Wilson

Thanks to Jen Williams for transcribing Jim's lectures on evangelism,
and to Lisa Just for putting them together as a book.

Unless otherwise stated, all Scripture quotations are from the New International Version, copyright © 1973, 1978, 1984, International Bible
Society. Used by permission of Zondervan. All rights reserved.

Cover design by David Dalbey. Illustrations by Forrest Dickison.
Interior design by Laura Storm. Layout by James Engerbretson.
Printed in the United States of America.

Library of Congress Cataloging-in-Publication Data
Library of Congress Cataloging-in-Publication Data
Wilson, James I.
  Taking men alive: evangelism on the front lines / Jim Wilson.
      ISBN 978-1-59128-132-0
  Witness bearing (Christianity) | Evangelistic work.
  LCC BV4520 .W527 2016
  DDC 269/.2--dc23
                                    2016026745

    16 17 18 19 20   9 8 7 6 5 4 3 2

Then he said to his disciples, "The harvest is plentiful but the workers are few. Ask the Lord of the harvest, therefore, to send out workers into his harvest field."

- Matthew 9:37-38

Also by the author
Principles of War
Weapons & Tactics
How to Be Free from Bitterness
Christ in Relationships DVD

CONTENTS

DEDICATION:

For men and women who are in the uttermost part of the earth turning people from the power of Satan to God.

All of the things in these chapters I have studied, meditated on, taught, and practiced for the last fifty years. Besides the Scriptures, I owe much of what you read to A. Paget Wilkes and his book *The Dynamic of Service*, a compilation of his teaching to missionaries gathered in Karuizawa, Japan, in 1920.

The title of this book has been taken from another book of the same title, published 1907. It was a book on evangelism by Charles G. Trumbull. It, in turn, was taken from a book by his father, Henry Clay Trumbull. Henry Clay Trumbull was a great personal evangelist in the last half of the nineteenth century. His book *Individual Work for Individuals* is a record of actual experiences, grouped by chronological periods in his life.

To "take alive" only occurs twice in the New Testament. "Then Jesus said to Simon, "Don't be afraid; from now on you will fish for people" (Luke 5:10).

The other is also evangelistic, only it is to set free, men who have been *taken alive* by Satan: "Opponents must be gently instructed, in the hope that God will grant them repentance leading them to a knowledge of the truth, and that they will come to their senses and escape from the trap of the devil, who has taken them captive to do his will" (II Timothy 2:25-26).

CHAPTER I

ACTS 26:18

Paul's testimony before Agrippa in Acts 26 gives key information about the principles of evangelism. Paul was appearing in trial before Festus after having been imprisoned by Felix for two years. When Paul came before Festus, he appealed to Caesar. Festus did not know what charges to write to Caesar concerning him, so he called on the king, Herod Agrippa, and the king's sister, Bernice. A few days later, the royal pair came with great pomp, and Paul was brought before them in chains.

The Apostle Paul had come a long way in his life up to that point. He had once been a great persecutor of the saints. Just before his conversion, the Lord spoke of him to Ananias, telling Ananias not to be afraid to go minister to him, saying, "This man is a chosen instrument to carry My name before the Gentiles and their kings and before the people of Israel" (Acts 9:15). Here was Paul, fulfilling the Lord's statement, appearing before Gentiles and their kings, though in chains. Yet there could be no doubt that Paul was in charge of the situation. He told the king and the governor how he had received his orders directly from Jesus Christ himself:

> On one of these journeys I was going to Damascus with the authority and commission of the chief priests. About noon, O King, as I was on the road, I saw a light from heaven, brighter than the sun, blazing around me and my companions. We all fell to the ground, and I heard a voice saying to me in Aramaic, "Saul, Saul, why do you persecute Me? It is hard for you to kick against the goads." Then I asked, "Who are you, Lord?" "I am Jesus, whom you are persecuting," the Lord replied. "Now get up and stand on your feet. I have appeared to you to appoint you as a servant and as a witness of what you have seen of Me and what I will show you. I will rescue you from your own people and from the Gentiles. *I am sending you to them to open their eyes and turn them from darkness to light, and from the power of Satan to God, so that they may receive forgiveness of sins and a place among those who are sanctified by faith in Me.*" (Acts 26:12-18, emphasis mine)

There is no greater authority than the Lord Jesus Christ. He gave the Great Commission to Paul personally. This was the greatest Teacher teaching the greatest student—Jesus telling Paul how to witness and to whom to witness. In this short speech before the king and the governor, Paul repeated the Great Commission to Herod in very significant detail.

> "*I am sending you to them to open their eyes and turn them from darkness to light, and from the power of Satan to God, so that they may receive forgiveness of sins and a place among those who are sanctified by faith in Me.*"

These are the two goals of evangelism: forgiveness of sins and an everlasting inheritance (a "place among those who are sanctified"). We are to expect these results from evangelism.

The Lord Jesus told Paul that to achieve these results, he must do three things: 1) open their eyes, 2) turn them from darkness to light, and 3) turn them from the power of Satan to God. As soon as people are turned from the power of Satan to God, they receive forgiveness and an everlasting inheritance.

These things are not equivalent to one another. They are three distinct, progressive elements of evangelism.

Let me illustrate. Suppose you are in a dark room with your eyes closed, and you say that you cannot see. I turn the light on. Do you see now? No. Why not? Because your eyes are closed! Light does not cause sight.

Suppose you are in a dark room again, with your eyes still closed. You say you cannot see, so I tell you to open your eyes. You open them, but you still can't see. Why? Because there is no light! Open eyes do not cause sight, either.

What Christ said to Paul makes sense when we think in terms of natural sight, light, and darkness. When we have our eyes closed, we naturally want darkness. But if we are in a dark room with our eyes wide open, we long for light. Closed eyes want darkness. Open eyes want light. Open eyes are *hungry* for light.

What we need in order to see is both elements: *open eyes and light*. The order here is important: the open eyes must come first. If you give light to a person whose eyes are still closed, the eyes just shut tighter. But if you open their eyes first and then give the light, they see and are glad to see.

The light is the gospel. The gospel is what turns people from darkness. John Chapter 1 tells us that the light was in the world, and the darkness could not put it out. It cannot overcome the light. That is wonderful! In 2 Corinthians 4:3-6, Paul reminds us that:

Even if our gospel is veiled, it is veiled to those who are
perishing. The god of this age has *blinded the minds* of the
unbelievers, so that they cannot see the light of the gospel of
the glory of Christ, who is the image of God. For we do not
preach ourselves, but Jesus Christ as Lord, and ourselves as
your servants for Jesus' sake. For God, who said, "Let light
shine out of darkness," made His light shine in our hearts
to give us the light of the knowledge of the glory of God in
the face of Christ.

The god of this world could not put out the light, but he
can blind the minds of those who do not believe—and he
has blinded them.

CHAPTER 2

OPENING EYES

The first element of evangelism is opening a person's eyes, that is, his desires, his sense of need. This is not done with the gospel. Because the gospel is the light, it must come only *after* the eyes are open. For hundreds of years Christians have been preaching the gospel to a pagan world whose eyes are shut. The world cannot see the light, because light does not cause sight.

Have you ever told the gospel to someone in complete detail, and after you finished, the person you talked with did not have the faintest understanding of what you had so carefully and clearly explained? Why did he not understand? His eyes were closed. Have you ever been in a church where they taught the gospel for two solid years in confirmation class, and at the end of all those classes the children were confirmed and never came back again? The church is under the impression that if it shines light on kids for two years, they will see. But they do not see, because light does not open eyes.

Several decades ago, I spent two years running a bookstore for a Missouri Synod Lutheran college. During that time, I asked many students if all the wonderful truth they had learned in confirmation class had sounded like good news to them. Most of them said, "Are you kidding? Two years of classes on Saturday mornings? Does that sound like good news to you?" Most of these students were preparing for the ministry, yet the gospel *still* did not sound like good news to them! I found only one student in that college who said, "Oh, yes, it was wonderful. I couldn't get enough of confirmation class." Someone had opened her eyes so that when she got the light, it looked like light.

Since giving light to someone with closed eyes does not make them understand, when you are opening people's eyes, you do not have to explain the gospel to them. They will not understand it, no matter how clearly you present it. *Opening eyes is not about making sense.* It is pre-light, pre-gospel. Opening eyes speaks to the need, the desire, the fears, the hunger, the thirst. The unbeliever does not need to understand at this point; he just needs to be left wanting *whatever* it is that will meet his need.

The Bible also speaks of evangelism in terms of farming. The book of Jeremiah tells us to break up the fallow ground. Jeremiah was speaking of spiritual ground here. The first step is to plow the hard ground, harrow it, soften it. Consider the Lord's parable of the sower from Mark chapter 4: A man went forth to sow, and some seed fell on the pathway, some fell on the rocks, some fell in the weeds, and some fell on good ground. Jesus said if the seed falls on the hard path, the birds eat it. It never gets inside; the devil takes it away. If it falls in the rocks, it does not have enough moisture and dies when the summer heat comes. If it falls in the weeds, the cares of the world choke it. But when it falls on good ground, it bears much fruit.

That is what would happen if you sowed that way. However, if Christ had been giving instruction on farming, He would not have said, "Go plant some seed on the turnpike." He would not say, "Go plant seed in the rocks." He would say, "Plow up the ground. Pick up the rocks, turn the soil over, get it ready for the seed." Opening eyes is like that. It is preparing the ground of a person's heart for the gospel. Plowed, soft hearts are hungry for seed just like open eyes are hungry for light. If we make someone hungry, when the seed of the gospel (which is the Word of God) is given, it is received. There may not be a conversion right away, but you will not run into an argument or an immediate rejection of the gospel. Then you can plant the seed and reap the harvest.

Suppose I have a thousand acres of unplowed ground that I want to be wheat. I say, "I need laborers in the field, so get out there!" and you run out, jump on a combine, and start driving it around the unplowed ground. I get you back and say, "No, no, wrong! Don't reap. Plow."

"What do you mean, 'Don't reap'? There were six stalks of wheat out there, and I got them all!"

You probably did. There are always people ready. However, when the ground is hard, we should plow. It is wonderful to watch the ground turn over. You know something? Hard ground does not object to being plowed. It only objects to being planted or reaped! Closed eyes do not object to being *opened*; they just object to being given light.

The best way to open a person's eyes is to live a godly life in front of him. He may not know what the cause of that godly life is, because that comes with his understanding of the gospel. Do not tell him why you live the life you do; you can tell him that after his eyes are open. He might think, "Oh, Joe is such a wonderful man. He must be a Buddhist. I think I'll study Buddhism." That is not bad, because he is still looking at you. Opening a person's eyes does not mean that he comes to God; it means that sooner or later he will come to *you* or to someone like you. When you live a godly life in front of people, it reaches them emotionally, either positively or negatively. It makes a person very conscious of his state, or perhaps just very conscious of *your* state. He realizes that he is unhappy with his, and he admires yours.

Living a godly life means having a great love for him. This love is not necessarily expressed with a gospel tract attached. (Remember, you are still opening eyes.) Love the person for who he is. Love him unconditionally, regardless of where he is. *Loving him* is key.

Another way to open eyes is with the things you say, in a testimony. This testimony does not have to have the gospel in it, either. Years ago, I was working in a Christian book-store in Ann Arbor, Michigan, and a student from the University of Michigan who had wandered in suddenly realized what kind of bookstore it was and felt obligated to tell me why she was not a Christian. She went through the entire history of Christianity—the Conquistadors, the Inquisition, the Crusades, the present inconsistency and hypocrisy of the Church, etc.

As she finished, I looked at her and said, "Well, that's funny. I don't agree with any of those things either, and I'm a Christian."

She looked at me, slightly puzzled. "How could that be?"

"I'll tell you why I'm a Christian." I said, "Twenty-three years ago I had an encounter with God that was like having a bath on the inside. It's changed my life, and I've been happy ever since. I'm sorry you're not a Christian." I turned around and started to walk away.

This woman was in a belligerent mood when she started talking to me. If I had presented the gospel to her, she would have fought back. Instead, I told her something that made her want more: I told her I had been happy for twenty-three years! I told her I was clean on the inside, but I did not tell her how I had gotten that way.

As I started to walk away, she grabbed me by the arm and said, "Aren't you going to tell me how this happened?"

I opened her eyes with a simple statement. If I had tried to give her light, it would not have worked. Just to be sure her eyes were open, I said, "Well, we do not believe in holding onto the customers."

She said, "I have all the time in the world." We went into the office, and I gave my testimony, this time loaded with the gospel. I gave her a whole stack of InterVarsity booklets. I do not know for certain that she ever became a Christian, but I am confident that she did. However, I do know this: her heart got plowed, and she got planted in good ground. That is all that had to happen! To push for the harvest right then would have been foolish. She was not ready. We do not have to always do the *whole thing* at once when we are evangelizing. Sometimes the seed needs time to grow before you can have a harvest.

Some biblical examples of this approach can be found in the Gospel of John. Look at John 3:2-3:

> He [Nicodemus] came to Jesus at night and said, "Rabbi, we know you are a teacher who has come from God. For no one could perform the miraculous signs you are doing if God were not with him." In reply Jesus declared, "I tell you

the truth, no one can see the kingdom of God unless he is born again."

That was the first time in the history of the world that the expression "born again" had been uttered.

Here is my question: Did Nicodemus know what Jesus was talking about? No! Did Jesus *know* that Nicodemus didn't know what He was talking about? Yes! Then why did He say it? Jesus was not communicating *information*. He was not communicating gospel. There was no light in His statement. Many people today think if you say "born again" often enough, you are preaching the gospel. There is *no gospel* in that statement. Jesus was not communicating light—He was communicating desire for the kingdom. He was opening Nicodemus' eyes. He kept laying it on, over and over. Finally, He rubbed it in: "You mean you are a teacher in Israel and you do not understand these things?"

Nicodemus was climbing the walls for light before it was over. Then Jesus gave it to him:

> Just as Moses lifted up the snake in the desert, so the Son of Man must be lifted up, that everyone who believes in Him may have eternal life. For God so loved the world that He gave His one and only Son, that whoever believes in Him shall not perish but have eternal life. For God did not send His Son into the world to condemn the world, but to save the world through Him. Whoever believes in Him is not condemned, but whoever does not believe stands condemned already because he has not believed in the name of God's one and only Son. (John 3:14-18)

Jesus set Nicodemus up. He opened his eyes, made him hungry, made him want more before He gave him the gospel.

The same thing occurred in John 4:

> When a Samaritan woman came to draw water, Jesus said
> to her, "Will you give me a drink?" (His disciples had gone
> into the town to buy food.) The Samaritan woman said to
> Him, "You are a Jew and I am a Samaritan woman. How
> can you ask me for a drink?" (For Jews do not associate with
> Samaritans.) (John 4:7-9)

This Samaritan woman had her eyes closed; she was unplowed ground.

> Jesus answered her, "If you knew the gift of God and who it
> is that asks you for a drink, you would have asked Him and
> He would have given you living water." "Sir," the woman
> said, "you have nothing to draw with and the well is deep.
> Where can you get this living water?" (John 4:10-11)

This woman simply did not know what Jesus was talking
about. Did Jesus know that? Yes. Then why did He say it?
He was making her *thirsty*. He was making her want.

> Jesus answered, "Everyone who drinks this water will be
> thirsty again, but whoever drinks the water I give them will
> never thirst. Indeed, the water I give them will become in
> them a spring of water welling up to eternal life." (John 4:13-
> 14)

Then she did not care where He got it.

> The woman said to him, "Sir, give me this water so that I
> won't get thirsty and have to keep coming here to draw wa-
> ter." (John 4:15).

She was still thinking of physical thirst. She was still
thinking of going out to the well with a jar. She did not
know what He was talking about, but she really wanted it.

When you are opening a person's eyes, the person does *not* have to understand what you are talking about. Jesus opened those two people's eyes: they did not understand Him, but they wanted whatever He was offering. After they wanted more, then He directed them to the light, to Himself. *"I who speak to you am He"* (John 4:26).

In both of these situations, Jesus had an important interim before He showed them the light. He told them the *bad news* first. In John Chapter 3 Jesus reminded Nicodemus of the serpent in the desert. People were dying—Nicodemus knew that. In Chapter 4, when the woman wanted the water, Jesus went through her sinful history first.

When you see someone amazed or astonished or in wonder, you can assume his eyes are open. This also happened at Lystra after a lame man was healed and the people began to bring the garlands to prepare a sacrifice to Paul and Barnabas as Hermes and Zeus (Acts 14:8-18). The people of Lystra had no idea what was going on, but their eyes were open. They were ready to listen because they thought Paul and Barnabas were something, even though they had the wrong view of who they were. When you see somebody who is in wonder or amazement about you or something the Lord has done, his eyes are open: go ahead and give him light.

Remember, if you try to give the gospel when the ground is hard, it will not get in. Let me tell you a story to illustrate. In 1964, right before Christmas, a girl walked into The Lamplighter Bookstore in College Park, Maryland. Hippies were not in great abundance yet, but she was the advance guard. I had not spoken to her, but I could see that as she walked around the store she was getting more and more turned off to what she was seeing. Finally, she headed for the door. I hated to have her leave with such a bad impression, so I cut her off, smiled, and said, "The books aren't that bad."

She said, "Like what?" which was not a great encouragement. I started out with C.S. Lewis. I talked C.S. Lewis—all kinds of C.S. Lewis. She was just champing at the bit to get away from me; she was not listening. I knew it, and I did not like her being that stubborn, so I got stubborn. This is where I was wrong. Instead of letting her go, I held on to her and tried more books. Finally I said, "We've got some great missionary biographies."

At that point, she blew her stack. "What do you mean going out there and putting clothes on those innocent people?!" She was angry.

Then I prayed to God for help. (I am always reminded of that passage in Nehemiah 2:4-5 when Nehemiah was the cupbearer to the king, and he had a sad countenance. Suddenly, the king asked him a question, and he was not up to the answer. Nehemiah said, "I *prayed* to the God of heaven and I *said* to the king...") Well, I prayed to the God of heaven. The Lord gave me help, and it was not the kind of help you could find in a book on personal evangelism. I suddenly thought of *The Savage, My Kinsman* by Elisabeth Elliot. It is a picture book on missions, and the last photo in the book is of an Auca Indian in his "nothing" strolling off into the woods with little Valerie Elliot, also in her "nothing." I took the book off the shelf and showed her the picture: "It looks more like the Indians are taking the clothes off the missionaries!"

She grabbed the book and said, "Let me see that!"

She sat down in a chair and started to read. She had been blind, but my statement and reading the book opened her eyes. I began to share the gospel with her. She took it in just like open eyes soak in light. A customer came in. I was afraid she would leave while I waited on the customer, so I gave her a little booklet called *Have You Considered Him?* She read it through. I came back and gave her more gospel. Another customer came in; I gave her another booklet. She stayed four hours. Her eyes were open; she got planted and she got reaped. At four o'clock in the afternoon she put her trust in the Lord Jesus.

Coming to the Lord does not always happen that fast: sometimes it happens over six months, sometimes many years. But it still follows the same pattern.

Another thing that opens eyes is your professional competence. Whatever you are—an engineer, a plumber, or a biologist—if you are a poor one, people who know you are a Christian will relate the two. They will attribute your poor performance to your Christianity. But when a Christian is competent in his profession, unbelievers also relate *that* to his Christianity. People will respect what you have in Christ if you are also doing well in your profession.

The things which open a person's eyes (or plow the ground) are a godly life, loving people, saying things that cause them to wonder or want, and giving your testimony (with or without the gospel in it). They are things that make people see that there is a difference between you and them, a difference they want to know more about.

CHAPTER 3

TURN THEM

From Darkness to Light

L et's go back to the passage from Acts 26 where Paul receives his commission from the Lord:

> For the Lord Jesus said to the Apostle Paul, "I have appeared to you to appoint you as a servant and as a witness of what you have seen of Me and what I will show you. I will rescue you from your own people and from the Gentiles. I am sending you to them to open their eyes and *turn them from darkness to light*, and from the power of Satan to God, so that they may receive forgiveness of sins and a place among those who are sanctified by faith in Me." (Acts 26:16-18)

This promise has two parts: the presentation, which is opening eyes, turning people from darkness to light, from the power of Satan to God, and the result, which is forgiveness of sins and an everlasting inheritance. As soon as people turn from the power of Satan unto God, they receive forgiveness and the everlasting inheritance.

As I mentioned before, the life you live in front of people is one of the things that opens eyes. But the gospel *lived* does not normally bring people to Christ. The gospel *proclaimed* does that. The gospel lived will create desire; the gospel proclaimed turns people to the light and begins a spiritual understanding of the gospel in them. Only after that does the will come in. First the hunger and desire, second, the spiritual comprehension of the gospel, and, third, the person's decision.

What is the gospel, and how do you present it? 1 Corinthians 15:1-5 is a good, succinct expression of the gospel. This is the light to give to opened eyes:

> Now, brothers, I want to remind you of the gospel I preached to you, which you received and on which you have taken your stand. By this gospel you are saved, if you hold firmly to the word I preached to you. Otherwise, you have believed in vain. (1 Cor. 15:1-2)

Paul makes it very clear that this is the gospel: "I preached it to you; you received it, you stand in it, you are saved by it." Then he tells us what the gospel is:

> For what I received I passed on to you as of first importance: that Christ died for our sins according to the Scriptures, that He was buried, that He was raised on the third day according to the Scriptures, and that He appeared to Peter, and then to the Twelve. (1 Cor. 15:3-5)

Paul tells us *the gospel is made up of these four things: the deity of Jesus Christ, His death for our sins, His burial, and His resurrection from the dead.*

To those of us who have been Christians a long time, these basic things can seem like old stuff. We hesitate to tell people about them because it sounds unnecessary or dogmatic since we have heard it many times. Yet it is *not* unnecessary, for this is the gospel proclaimed.[1] When we have opened a person's eyes and want to give light, this is the light we must give. You could assume that people from the West have already gotten light someplace in our Christianized culture, but I believe it is wrong to make that assumption. If they received light in the past, it might have been before their eyes were open. So once a person's eyes are open, be sure to give him the light of the gospel.

This little gospel "formula" of the deity, death, burial, and resurrection of Jesus Christ shows up repeatedly in the book of Acts. It is preached in the message prior to each time someone is converted.

Look at the story of Cornelius in Acts 10:34. Cornelius' eyes are already open. They had been opened, not by Peter, but probably years before as he searched for the truth. They were certainly opened wide when an angel appeared in all his glory in Cornelius' room. When Peter arrived, he said to Cornelius,

> I now realize how true it is that God does not show favoritism but accepts men from every nation who fear Him and do what is right. You know the message God sent to the people of Israel, telling the good news of peace through *Jesus Christ, who is Lord of all.* (Acts 10:34-36)

That is the first part of the gospel—who Christ is. He is Lord of all.

> You know what has happened throughout Judea, beginning in Galilee after the baptism that John preached—how God anointed Jesus of Nazareth with the Holy Spirit and power,

---

1. This does not include repentance, because repentance is not part of the gospel. The gospel or good news is what Jesus Christ did. Repentance is man's response to the gospel.

and how He went around doing good and healing all who were under the power of the devil, because God was with Him. We are witnesses of everything He did in the country of the Jews and in Jerusalem. *They killed Him by hanging Him on a tree.* (Acts 10:37-39)

The second point: Christ died.

But God raised Him from the dead on the third day and caused Him to be seen. (Acts 10:40)

The third point: He was raised from the dead. Christ's burial is not mentioned explicitly here; it is assumed with the death and resurrection. The reason the burial is placed in 1 Corinthians 15 is because the burial confirms His death. You have heard the expression "dead and buried." When someone says a person is "dead and buried," it means he is dead-dead. He is really, truly, irrevocably dead. There is no possibility of artificial resuscitation. Christ's burial confirms His death, and it also confirms His resurrection. It was His *body* that was not there. The burial is very clearly a part of the good news: dead and buried, buried and risen. We can sometimes leave it out, if we make it clear from the resurrection that the burial was not bypassed.

"But God raised Him from the dead on the third day and caused Him to be seen. He was not seen by all the people, but by witnesses whom God had already chosen—by us who ate and drank with Him after He rose from the dead. He commanded us to preach to the people and to testify that He is the one whom God appointed as judge of the living and the dead. All the prophets testify about Him that everyone who believes in Him receives forgiveness of sins through His name." *While Peter was still speaking* these words, the Holy Spirit came on all who heard the message. The circumcised believers who had come with Peter were astonished that the gift of the Holy Spirit had been poured out even on the Gentiles. (Acts 10:40-45)

The proclamation of the deity, the death, and the resurrection of Christ is *absolutely essential*. As soon as Peter had gotten through the minimum of gospel truth and as soon as he said what a person had to do, the Holy Spirit saved all those people. They were so hungry for the gospel that the Holy Spirit could have bypassed the trip to Joppa to get Peter. The angel could have told them the good news, but he did not. He chose to use a man to bring these people to Him. Peter did not even get to the invitation. "While Peter was still speaking these words…."

Look at Acts 2 and 3. In Acts 2, the rushing, mighty wind and the disciples speaking in tongues opened the eyes of the people. Verse 12:

Amazed and perplexed, they asked one another, "What does this mean?"

When a person is amazed and perplexed, it is very likely his eyes are open. Those people heard the disciples speaking in their own tongues the wonderful works of God. I doubt if it was the gospel the disciples were speaking, but rather all the other wonders of God. Peter stood up, and before he preached the gospel, he identified with the people by quoting from the Old Testament, from Joel 2:28-32:

And afterward,
    I will pour out my Spirit on all people.
Your sons and daughters will prophesy,
    your old men will dream dreams,
    your young men will see visions.

Even on my servants, both men and women,
   I will pour out my Spirit in those days.
I will show wonders in the heavens
   and on the earth,
   blood and fire and billows of smoke.
The sun will be turned to darkness
   and the moon to blood
   before the coming of the great and dreadful day of
   the LORD.
And everyone who calls
   on the name of the LORD will be saved;
for on Mount Zion and in Jerusalem
   there will be deliverance,
   as the LORD has said,
even among the survivors
   whom the LORD calls.

This was further opening of their eyes. Once Peter had their attention, he spoke this:

> Men of Israel, listen to this: Jesus of Nazareth was a man accredited by God to you by miracles, wonders and signs, which God did among you through Him, as you yourselves know. This man was handed over to you by God's set purpose and foreknowledge, and you, with the help of wicked men, put Him to death by nailing Him to the cross. But God raised Him from the dead, freeing Him from the agony of death, because it was impossible for death to keep its hold on Him. (Acts 2:22-24)

Then Peter went through the Old Testament Scriptures establishing that the Messiah was Lord and was prophesied to rise from the dead. He told the people that Jesus had died and risen again; therefore He was the Messiah and Lord. He ended up in verse 36 with:

> Therefore let all Israel be assured of this: God has made this Jesus, whom you crucified, both Lord and Christ (Acts 2:36).

Peter gave the deity of Jesus Christ, His death, and His resurrection. This was the light. As soon as the gospel was preached, the people were no longer amazed and perplexed.

> They were cut to the heart and said…"Brothers, what shall we do?" (Acts 2:37b)

At this point, they were ready to be turned from the power of Satan to God. Peter gave them the answer.

> Peter replied, "Repent and be baptized, every one of you, in the name of Jesus Christ for the forgiveness of your sins. And you will receive the gift of the Holy Spirit. The promise is for you and your children and for all who are far off—for all whom the Lord our God will call." With many other words he warned them; and he pleaded with them, "Save yourselves from this corrupt generation." Those who accepted his message were baptized, and about three thousand were added to their number that day. (Acts 2:38-41)

In Acts 3, there is a different means of opening the people's eyes. This is the story of the healing of the man at the Beautiful Gate of the temple.

> Then Peter said, "Silver or gold I do not have, but what I have I give you. In the name of Jesus Christ of Nazareth, walk." Taking him by the right hand, he helped him up, and instantly the man's feet and ankles became strong. He jumped to his feet and began to walk. Then he went with them into the temple courts, walking and jumping, and praising God.

When all the people saw him walking and praising God, they recognized him as the same man who used to sit begging at the temple gate called Beautiful, and *they were filled with wonder and amazement* at what had happened to him. (Acts 3:6-10)

That opened their eyes! Then Peter began the gospel in verse 13:

Men of Israel...The God of Abraham, Isaac, and Jacob, the God of our Fathers, has glorified His servant Jesus. You handed Him over to be killed, and you disowned Him before Pilate, though he had decided to let Him go. You disowned the Holy and Righteous One and asked that a murderer be released to you. *You killed the author of life, but God raised Him from the dead.* (Acts 3:13-15a)

That is short, but *powerful*. It gave light to the open eyes. Peter never got to turn the people from the power of Satan to God, because the apostles were locked up before they were finished. However, they were turned without Peter:

But many of who heard the message believed, and the number of men grew to about five thousand. (Acts 4:4)

This is the pattern throughout the book of Acts. Whenever Peter gets to the gospel, he states it just as briefly as in 1 Corinthians 15. Most of the time there is a preamble, an identification with the people, or something else to get their attention and open their eyes, but once Peter begins the gospel, he lays it on fast.

How the gospel is delivered is very important. The disciples delivered it filled with the Holy Spirit. They also delivered it with great boldness, and when they did not have boldness, they asked God for it. Moreover, "great grace" was upon them all. Lastly, they were of one heart and soul, one accord. The apostles declared the truth unapologetically, with great love, grace, power, and boldness, and people responded.

Many Christians have gotten the idea that if you present the gospel directly it is wrong. We picture someone coming up to a person on the street corner, grabbing him by the shirt collar, and saying, "Brother, are you saved?" We have fallen into the trap of thinking that directness is unkind and harsh. The apostles were direct in the book of Acts, but they were neither harsh nor unloving. If you *love* people, you can be direct. If you do not love people, all the tact in the world will not help you, because they will still see that you do not love them. *Tact is not the substitute for harshness.* When we are direct and loving at the same time, our message will not be rejected because of our directness, although it may be rejected because the gospel itself can be a stumbling block. The gospel *does* turn people off. We do not want that, so sometimes we avoid directness or even avoid the gospel itself. This is not right. We need to be direct with the gospel; there is no other way we can truly present it. Peter was more than direct about Christ dying for our sins. He said, "You are the ones who, with the help of wicked men, put Him to death by nailing Him to the cross" (Acts 2). When it is time to present the gospel, we should not beat around the bush.

Another common problem is thinking that we are giving the gospel when we are not actually. Let me share a few experiences to illustrate.

My family and I were at one time members of a congregation in Washington, D.C. One day, I was talking with the pastor on the front lawn of the church. He said to me, "Jim, I preached my heart out all year and had no converts. Now in the last six weeks we have had seventeen people receive Christ. I do not understand it. Why have I not had any response all year but seventeen in the last six weeks?"

The last six weeks had been the six weeks before Easter, so the pastor had decided to preach on the cross. It was that simple. I said, "You preached the gospel the last six weeks; the rest of the year you did not preach it."

Another time there was a week of evangelistic meetings at the church we attended in Annapolis, Maryland. The man who came to speak was the brother of a famous evangelist. All week he spoke with great enthusiasm and exuberance, with all the mannerisms and terminology of a talented evangelist—but no gospel. He spoke with great (I would almost say "natural") power, but night after night he left the gospel out! For the life of me, I could not see how he could do it. Finally, near the end of the week, I spoke to him and told him he was not preaching the gospel. It did not make any difference: the next few nights he still did not preach it. The meetings came to an end, and the evangelist asked the pastor from the Edgewater Baptist Church to give the final benediction. Lynn Royston stood up and prayed the entire gospel of Jesus Christ. Afterwards, I could hardly get to him fast enough. I shook his hand and said, "I appreciated the gospel." He said, "I know. I've missed it all week, too."

If you are a pastor, I am not saying you should preach the gospel every time you give a sermon or every time you speak at a church meeting. But do not think you are preaching it if you are not, and do not expect commitments to Jesus Christ without the gospel. Who Christ is, His death for our sins, His burial, and His resurrection from the dead: *that* is the gospel.

At the Naval Academy we had an annual banquet during Graduation Week. The purpose of the banquet was to have the gospel preached to the parents, girlfriends, and guests of the graduating midshipmen. The year that I was in charge of the banquet I invited an old man, a very famous personal evangelist who could go into the office of a newly-elected senator and say, "Young man, are you here in the will of God?"

The senator would look at him and say, "I don't know."

He would reply, "You mean you are a senator of the United States and you don't know whether you're in the will of God?" Then he would proclaim the gospel. He had a gift of loving directness. I phoned and asked him if he would preach the gospel at the Graduation Week banquet. I said, "If there's any negative reaction, we'll take it; we will be glad to take it. We think the ground has been plowed, and we want it planted. Make it very clear."

He said, "I understand completely."

The banquet was in St. Anne's parish hall. The acoustics were bad, it was a hot night, and there was much noise from the kitchen. Bessie and I prayed that he would preach the gospel.

The evangelist was at the head table. He was conscious that he was going to be hard to hear. He must have been close to eighty years old at the time, but when he was introduced, he climbed up on a chair and stood on the banquet table! He said, "Let's all stand and sing 'Blessed Assurance, Jesus is Mine.'" He led everyone in the song. Then he really, really plowed the ground. He opened many eyes. He got everyone listening to every word he said, made them really hungry for what he was going to say. Then he moved from plowing the ground to reaping the harvest, and *he did not preach the gospel.* There was no harvest. My wife Bessie and I sat there sick. No gospel, no deity of Jesus Christ, no death for our sins, no resurrection from the dead. The trouble is that I am sure he *thought* he had preached it. In Christian work, we can very easily center on certain things and think that we are preaching the gospel when we are not preaching it at all.

Before Corrie ten Boom became famous, when she was in her early seventies, she visited us for a week in Annapolis. Instead of everyone coming to see her, we had to take her to see them. She spoke seventeen times in that week. When the week was over, I took her to the airport. In the car, she said, "Jim, I know that God gave me the gift of evangelism in Australia. Many, many people came to know the Savior in Australia. But since I came to the United States, there have not been conversions. Do you think that God took away the gift of evangelism?"

I said, "No, Corrie. In Romans 11 it says 'The gifts and calling of God are without repentance.' God doesn't take away gifts. But it is not the gift of evangelism that saves. It is the gospel. I listened to you seventeen times this week, and you didn't mention the gospel once. The closest you got was talking about the nail prints in His hand. You really helped many of the Christians, and you taught a lot of truth, but you did not preach the gospel."

I do not know why this happens. It may be because we are not spiritually alert. It may be that the enemy is keeping us from speaking things that will get through to people's hearts. When the gospel comes through clear and the message gets down inside, you are going to get a response. People have to say "yes" to Jesus Christ or they have to say "no" to Him, and sometimes they do not like to make that choice. When you open their eyes, you get only "Yeses," because people like having their eyes opened.

Even if you present it at the right time and in the right way, some people will still reject the gospel.

> Jews demand signs and Greeks look for wisdom, but we preach Christ crucified: a *stumbling block* to Jews and *foolishness* to Gentiles. (1 Cor. 1:22-23)

> Brothers and sisters, if I am still preaching circumcision, why am I still being persecuted? In that case *the offense of the cross* has been abolished. (Gal. 5:11)

Every place that the Apostle Paul had a revival, he also had a riot. The gospel is not neutral.

Plant the gospel after the person's eyes are open, when he is plowed and soft. One of the ways you can tell that a person is ready to be planted is the things he says. Of course, he will not come up to you and say, "I have been plowed. I am ready to be planted." On the contrary—he will try to keep you thinking he is in the same position he always was. People can even be belligerent at this point because "men loved darkness rather than light because their deeds were evil" (John 3:19b).

Some people do not even want their eyes opened because they know that light changes, and they do not want to be changed. However, most people who are hard ground do not know enough to be antagonistic. The antagonism comes after they have been planted, when it is time to make a decision. The man with closed eyes is generally apathetic about Christianity. It is alright for him to have Christians around; it is nice—they are good for the community. He is tolerant. That means you have not gotten to him yet.

Once you have opened his eyes by loving him, showing kindness to him, and living a godly life in front of him, he will begin to wonder what makes you tick. Then he will come up with a statement like, "Well, if I ever become a Christian…" That first "if" means he is plowed. He is asking for the gospel. Later on, he might say, "Well, maybe in five years," or "Before I die, I will become a Christian…" He has just gone from "if" to "when." This tells you several things. He knows that he is a sinner and needs a savior. He knows that Jesus Christ is the Son of God, that He died for our sins and rose again from the dead. He is thinking of *when* he is going to commit his life to Christ. That means that he knows that the gospel is true and that he needs it. Once he speaks of "when," do not spend any more time giving the gospel. He is ready to turn from the power of Satan to God.

Years ago, there was a young mother in our church who had been taking care of the nursery for several years. Finally, she said, "I'm up to here with little kids. I'm going to get into an adult class." She joined my wife Bessie's Sunday school class. She was there for one day and realized that she was not a Christian.

This woman lived two blocks from us and often took her little girls for walks. The next day, she walked back and forth in front of our house, hoping Bessie would come out with our son Gordon in the stroller so she could tell Bessie she was not a Christian. She was about to give up when Bessie finally came out. Bessie tried to assure her that she was a Christian, but it became evident that she was not. Bessie led her to the Lord. She was ripe for harvest. She went home a new person. Her new life opened the eyes of her husband. Over the next few weeks I gave him the light of the gospel.

One day, the wife came back to Bessie and said, "You'd better not have Jim come over anymore. Fred is about ready to punch him in the nose." Good sign! That meant he was ready to turn. What condition was the Apostle Paul in the instant before he was converted? Antagonistic! He was ripe, even though he did not look it to Ananias. So I went over to Fred's house to get punched in the nose. As I went through the last of the gospel, Fred said, "Well, Jim, maybe in five years I will become a Christian."

You cannot think in terms of "when" for that long. Imagine you are engaged to be married. You have just proposed, the girl said "Yes," and you say, "Let's set a date five years from now." You cannot think in terms of "when" for five years. It is the same with the gospel. When a man is talking of "when," the "when" will be soon.

I went home rejoicing, confident that Fred would be a Christian within a week. That Sunday at church, he and I were assigned to count the money together after the service. We were counting on opposite sides of the table, and he said, "Jim, you'd better come over this afternoon. I think I'm ready."

These are a few of the ways you can tell when someone is ready to move to the next step. However, it is not cut-and-dried. You generally will keep on opening eyes then planting seed, and planting seed then reaping the harvest, moving *gradually* from one stage to the next; but you need to know whether you are early in the planting or almost ready for the harvest.

There are only four types of non-Christians in this world: unplowed, unplanted, unripened, and unreaped. It is important to know that there is usually a waiting period between the planting and the reaping. Back when you were in kindergarten, your teacher might have sent you home with a bean and told you if you planted it, it would grow. You took it home and planted it in the yard. You went out the next day and did not see anything growing, so you dug up the bean to see what was wrong. Then you put it back in the ground. The next day, nothing had happened, so you dug up the bean again to check on it. You did this every day, and somehow the bean never *did* grow.

The same thing often happens with planting the gospel. We plant someone, then we feel obligated to go dig them up the next day to see if they are growing. If you plant the gospel in good ground, *wait*. Go plant someone else! Do not dig the first one up. Keep on plowing and planting and plowing and planting, and soon you will be reaping all of the time.

> He that sows sparingly shall reap sparingly. He who sows abundantly shall reap abundantly. (2 Cor. 9:6)

The Apostle Paul was speaking about giving money in this verse, but I think the principle applies to evangelism, too. The more gospel you plant, the more harvest there will be.

In this country there has been a lot of gospel planted on hard ground. Yet there are some works like Young Life that are experts at plowing (opening eyes). In Young Life clubs they plow every week, and they plant every week. Young Life turns out to be a holding pattern for kids until they go to a Young Life camp; then they get hit with "believe and repent" and come back converted. The problem with this is not everybody goes to camp. As a result, Young Life produces many, many plowed and planted people, but not as many reaped ones. But they are great at opening people's eyes. I know one Young Life club leader who said, "If there are 100 kids in this room next week, I'll shave my legs." How many kids do you think he had at the meeting the next week? About 110. What does shaving his legs have to do with the gospel? Absolutely nothing! But it sure opened their eyes. It made them willing to listen to anything he said.

InterVarsity is expert on the gospel. Campus Crusade dwells on the reaping. If we wanted to reach this country for Christ, it would be very simple. Send everyone to Young Life, bring in InterVarsity to lay the gospel on, then call in Campus Crusade to reap the harvest. But we cannot do this. We need to recognize for ourselves what kind of ground people are because we may be the only ones farming.

The groups I mentioned are experts in their different fields, and each one of them has results. But each is also prone to think it has discovered the means by which we can reach the world. What did the Apostle Paul say?

> I have become all things to all men, if by all means I might save some. (1 Cor. 9:22b)

Paul did not say he had *the* means of reaching everyone, but that he used *all* means to reach *some* of them. We should be versatile so that we can do all three of these things: recognize where a person is, plow and rest with that, plant and rest with that. There are enough unsaved people in this world for you to work somewhere else while the plowed ground and the planted ground are resting and growing. If you plant in good ground, the person will be convicted. He might not turn to Christ, but there will come a time when he *can*.

I use books to evangelize. There are certain books that plow the ground, certain books that plant the seed, and certain books that reap the harvest. I do not always give the same kind of book to every person. *The Chronicles of Narnia*[2] is good for plowing, even though there is some gospel in it. A number of years ago, there was a freshman girl named Carolyn whose older sister had come to Christ in our noon Bible studies. The sister brought Carolyn to the study for a while. One day she came into the bookstore and announced to me that she had decided not to become a Christian.

I said, "Well, tell me about it."

She told me why not, and then she said, "If Jesus were like the Lion, I'd become a Christian right now." The Chronicles of Narnia is an eye-opener. She had gotten a greater picture of the gospel and the love of God through this fictional character than she had ever received at the church she grew up in. She had a distorted view of the person and character of Jesus Christ.

I said, "He is more like the Lion than the Lion is!" She received Christ that day.

If people like C.S. Lewis, give them *The Screwtape Letters*. If they like that, give them *The Great Divorce*, then *Mere Christianity*. As they follow the author through the books, they get more and more of the gospel.

One day a young hermit from out in the mountains came into our bookstore in Moscow, Idaho. He had come to town to buy some occult books, but the only other bookstore was closed, so he ended up at Crossroads. One of our staff mem-

2. This is a series of seven fairy tales written by C.S. Lewis. They are children's books, but ones that adults like to read—adventure stories that are fast moving and have all kinds of wild things in them. In each of these books, there comes a point of clear conversion and the very clear cost of it. In the first book, *The Lion, the Witch and the Wardrobe*, the lion, who represents Christ in all of the books, dies for Edmund's sin and rises from the dead. As you read this to little children, they are in tears when he is killed and rejoicing when he rises from the dead.

bers, Barbara Friedman, loaned him two books: *The Cross and the Switchblade* by David Wilkerson to open his eyes and *Basic Christianity* by John Stott to give him the gospel. She figured if he was out in the mountains awhile, he would read the one and then the other, get plowed and planted, and come back ready to receive the Lord.

When he returned several weeks later, Barbara was busy talking to one of her converts, and I was on the telephone. Another of our staff members, Nancy Greensides, was the only one not with someone, but she was back in the office. This guy walked to the rear of the store and very loudly announced, "I've come to return these books!" But we were all busy, so we could not pay attention to him. He walked back to the front and put the books on the counter. I thought he was going to walk out, but he turned and walked to the rear again. I went up to the counter to see which books he had left.

I asked, "Did you like the books?"

He said, still very loudly, "Well, *The Cross and the Switchblade* wasn't much, but that *Basic Christianity* really got to me."

I asked him if he would like to talk with someone, and he said he would. Nancy took him down to the reading room and led him to the Lord. I knew that he had been plowed and planted, and he was saying, "I want to be reaped." He was really ready.

If you have been encouraged that you can open people's eyes, and that fits your personality better than preaching the gospel, remember—once you get his eyes open you still have to give the gospel! You are not off the hook. You can say, "Well, I'm a plower. Someone else can plant him." But what if no one is around to plant? Are you going to plow him

forever? You need to be willing to plow, to plant, and to reap.
It is an easy thing to do when people want to be planted and
want to be reaped.

CHAPTER 4

TURN THEM

from the Power of Satan to God

In Matthew 9, when Jesus saw the multitudes and had compassion on them, He said,

> The harvest is plentiful, but the workers are few. Ask the Lord of the harvest, therefore, to send out workers into His harvest field. (Matt. 9:37-38)

Jesus does not say there is unplowed ground. He does not say there is unplanted ground. He says there is a *harvest*. When He sends out laborers, He does not send out plowers. He does not send out planters. He asks us to pray that the Lord of the *harvest* would send out *reapers*. The expression "go to the harvest fields" is often used in reference to the mission field. However, in most cases, the mission fields are not harvest fields yet. They have not even been plowed. Yet because Jesus says He wants laborers to go into the harvest, we can infer that there is a harvest ready *now*, and we are to pray that the Lord would send out laborers into it.

There are several verbs that describe what happens between the sinner and the Savior at the harvest. They are not synonyms in the dictionary, but they are synonyms in action. One of these is the word *believe*. Belief is not passive. It is an action.

> Whoever *believes* in Him shall not perish but have eternal life. (John 3:16)

> Yet to all who *received* Him, to those who *believed* in His name, He gave the right to become the children of God. (John 1:12)

The emphasis in the second verse is on the connection between receiving and believing. It is almost as if *receiving* Jesus is a more explicit description of the action that takes place when you believe.

Another synonym is the word *repent*. This one comes up often, both in the Old and the New Testaments. *Repent* is also an action:

> And when they had come to him, he said to them: "You know, from the first day that I came to Asia, in what manner I always lived among you…testifying to Jews, and also to Greeks, *repentance* toward God and faith toward our Lord Jesus Christ." (Acts 20:18, 21)

There is a connection between *receiving* and *believing*, and between *repentance* and *faith*. What is the connection? The object of each of these verbs is the Lord Jesus Christ. We believe in *Him*. We receive *Him*. We repent toward *Him*. We have faith in *Him*.

There is another verb in Jesus' wonderful invitation in Matthew 11:28:

Come to Me, all you who are weary and burdened, and I will give you rest.

The verb is *come*. Who is the object? Jesus Christ. "Come *to Me*." Receiving, repenting, coming, believing, and having faith in are all the same action, to the same person.

There is another word for this action—one that we avoid. It is the word *obey*. The reason we avoid it is that we know "works-righteousness" is wrong, and we have connected *works* with *obedience,* and thus *obedience* with *works-righteousness*. We do not want to be guilty of works-righteousness, so we are not going to be guilty of *obedience*, either. I am not talking about obedience in terms of living the Christian life on a day-to-day basis; I am talking about that basic obedience, right at the beginning. In Acts 17:30-31, when Paul was addressing the people of Athens, he said:

> In the past God overlooked such ignorance, but now *He commands all people everywhere to repent.* For He has set a day when He will judge the world with justice by the man He has appointed. He has given proof of this to all men by raising Him from the dead.

What has God said? "But now He *commands* all people everywhere to repent." Repentance is one of the salvation verbs. But God has also *commanded* it. So when a person repents, what has he done? He has *obeyed* God's command. In other words, the invitation to receive Christ is not just an invitation: God "*commands* all people everywhere" to come to Him.

I spent eleven years in the Navy, and one thing I discovered there was that you do not have to do what you are told. You do not *have* to obey commands. But if you don't, they sure can make you wish you had! It is the same here. God has commanded all people everywhere to repent. Men can choose to disobey, but repentance is not a suggestion, not an invitation. Of course, there is also an invitation, when *we* give it. 2 Corinthians 5:20 says, "We implore you on Christ's behalf: be reconciled to God." That is expressed as a request. Yet even so, it is a request with all the authority of Jesus Christ. "We implore you on *Christ's behalf.*" We are speaking for the Lord Jesus Christ, and behind this authority is the complete provision of the gospel—Jesus Christ *died* for all men, so He has no hesitancy to *command* all men.

> Although He was a son, He learned *obedience* from what He suffered, and, once made perfect, He became the source of eternal salvation for all who *obey* Him. (Hebrews 5:8-9)

This obedience is not works-righteousness; it is obedience to the command to repent. Jesus became the author of salvation to all those who *obey* Him by *believing and repenting.*

> God is just: He will pay back trouble to those who trouble you and give relief to you who are troubled, and to us as well. This will happen when the Lord Jesus is revealed from heaven in blazing fire with His powerful angels. He will punish those who do not know God and do not *obey* the gospel of our Lord Jesus. (2 Thess. 1:6-8)

The good news is something to be obeyed. God will deal with those who do not know Him, who have not *obeyed* the gospel.

These words have been in front of us all the time. Because we are afraid of being accused of preaching salvation by works, we have stayed away from these salvation texts. However, obedience to the gospel is not works-righteousness.

Let us look at the greatest book on justification in the New Testament—Romans.

Paul, a servant of Christ Jesus, called to be an apostle and set apart for the gospel of God—the gospel He promised beforehand through His prophets in the Holy Scriptures regarding His Son, who as to His human nature was a descendant of David, and who through the Spirit of holiness was declared with power to be the Son of God by His resurrection from the dead: Jesus Christ our Lord. Through Him and for His name's sake, we received grace and apostleship to call people from among all the Gentiles to *the obedience that comes from faith.* (Rom. 1:1-5)

At the very beginning of his book on justification by faith, Paul uses the expression "the obedience that comes from faith." Look at the way the book ends:

Now to Him who is able to establish you by my gospel and the proclamation of Jesus Christ, according to the revelation of the mystery hidden for long ages past, but now revealed and made known through the prophetic writings by *the command of the eternal God*, so that all nations might *believe and obey* Him. (Rom. 16:25-26)

The command to obey is not just any command: it is the command of the *gospel*.

The Old Testament character who is mentioned most often in the New Testament is Abraham. Look at what Hebrews 11:8 says about him:

By *faith* Abraham, when called to go to a place he would later receive as his inheritance, *obeyed and went.*

Now look back at verse 7:

By *faith* Noah, when warned about things not yet seen, in holy fear *built an ark* to save his family. By his faith he condemned the world and became heir of the righteousness that comes by faith.

What did Noah do? He built an ark. Suppose he was told to do this, and he said, "God, I believe You. You know I have never doubted You. I have complete faith in You. But if You think I'm going to build a boat in this desert, You're crazy!" Would he have been saved? Not at all. There was no way Noah could have had faith *without building the ark.* This is an example of faith that requires obedience. As you look through Hebrews 11, you will see again and again the strong connection between faith and obedience, between faith and action.

As I understand it from talking with Wycliffe Bible translators, when they come into language groups with a very limited vocabulary, they have a hard time translating the word "believe." It is an abstract word, and peoples with limited vocabularies do not have abstracts. So the translators put in the word "obey" instead, because it is the closest thing they can come up with. It does not occur to them that they are teaching works-righteousness, because they are not. People *do* obey the gospel.

There is one more verb connection. Look at Romans 10:

> But what does it say? "The word is near you; it is in your mouth and in your heart," that is, *the word of faith* we are proclaiming: That if you *confess* with your mouth, "Jesus is Lord," and *believe* in your heart that God raised Him from the dead, you will be saved. For it is with your heart that you *believe* and are justified, and it is with your mouth that you *confess* and are saved. As the Scripture says, "Anyone who trusts in him will never be put to shame." For there is no difference between Jew and Gentile—the same Lord is Lord of all and

richly blesses all who call on Him, for, *"Everyone who calls on the name of the Lord* will be saved." (Rom. 10:8-13)

The new verbs are "confess" and "call." "Confess" expresses belief. "Calling" is the action that accompanies confession. Paul uses it in his testimony in Acts 22 when he recounts how Ananias came to see him:

> A man named Ananias came to see me. He was a devout observer of the law and highly respected by all the Jews living there. He stood beside me and said, "Brother Saul, receive your sight!...And now what are you waiting for? Get up, be baptized and wash your sins away, *calling on his name.*" (Acts 22:12-13a, 16)

And he did.

If the connections between these verbs tells us anything, it is that conversion is an event that takes place *between the sinner and the Savior,* not between the sinner and the church or the sinner and a saint *about* the Savior. True expressions *about* the Savior do not save. What saves is the transaction that takes place *with* Him.[3] If you have plowed and planted and think someone is ready, what he needs is to have a transaction with the Lord. First, he should have as complete a knowledge as you can express with Scripture about the Person to whom he is turning. He should know, as completely as he can, who Jesus Christ is. He should know His death for our sins, His burial, and His resurrection from the dead. Before you give him the command to repent, there should be no doubt about whom he is turning to and why he should turn to Him.

3. Did you notice the gospel in these different passages? It does not occur completely in every one, but each passage emphasizes who the Lord is and sometimes the crucifixion and the resurrection.

There may be a problem with what he is turning *from*. Most people in sin do not realize how much sin they are in until after they are converted. People who come to the Lord generally do not come to Him for all of the problems they have but just for one or two that they are conscious of and which are troubling them. That is why trying to get someone to comprehend the dozens of problems that you see in his life so that he can turn away from them is generally a mistake. However, if he turns to God for the thing he knows is a problem, the Lord will save him from everything. (Unless of course, he deliberately says, "Well, Lord, I only want to be saved from this one thing, and I would like to keep the rest of it.") Teach him to turn to the Lord with no reservations. When a man does this, Christ takes care of everything. Matthew 11:28 says: *"Come to Me, all you who are weary and burdened…"* Jesus was saying, "You can come to Me with burdens. You do not have to recognize all your individual sins." The object is to come to the Father by the Lord Jesus.

One fellow I met used to take his little boy to Sunday school and then go across the street to the drug store and drink coffee until Sunday school was over. One week, some-one from the church asked him what he did during Sunday school.

"Well, I go across to Reed's Drug Store and drink coffee."

"They serve free coffee in the adult Sunday school class. Why don't you wait it out there?"

I had been asked to teach the adult Sunday school that week. With the exception of the regular Sunday school teacher, I did not know anyone in the class. She had invited me to teach the gospel, so I assumed there had been some plowing done. This fellow was there in class for the first time, drinking coffee. I came on strong with the gospel, and it hit him hard. Three weeks later I received a phone call from him.

"You don't know who I am. I heard you three weeks ago in a Sunday school class. That night I was putting my little boy to bed. He's the kind of kid that you have to stay in the room with or he's out of bed immediately. I was standing guard in the room, and I thought, 'Since I'm here, I might as well pray for Guy.' I prayed for Guy, but something happened to me. I don't know what it is, but I need an explanation. I've gone to the same bar five nights a week for the last thirteen years. Now I'm only going one night a week, and that's to bowl. That's not the funny part, though: I love beer, but I'm ordering Coca-Cola and I don't know why! That's not all. I used to be so profane that it didn't make any difference if it was in front of my wife, my mother, or in a public place. I never paid attention to what I was saying; the words were just automatic. Restaurant managers would have to ask me to tone it down because I would scare away their customers. But now if I say one bad word, I want to bite my tongue off, and everyone else that works with me has suddenly become so profane I can hardly stand it."

This man had come to the Lord for his little boy, but he came with no reservations, and the Lord cleaned up the whole house. If I had previously tried to talk with him about his profanity, it would not have made sense to him. Find out where each person is likely to hurt and hit him there. Get him where he is vulnerable, and let the Lord take care of the rest.

There was a woman named Colette who came to the Lord during a Bible study in our home in Yokohama. She had a sister named Arlette. They were French Algerian and had both married American Army officers during the war. They had grown up in a Catholic convent school, but they described themselves as atheists. Colette asked my wife and me to look up her sister in Washington, DC, but Arlette was not interested in meeting with us.

Then one day she called. She had melanoma on her ankle. She was ready for the gospel, not because she was weighed down by sins, but because she was in physical need. She received Christ.

Six weeks later, she called and said, "Jim, when I became a Christian, I had no intention of becoming a bigot."

I said, "I had no intention of you becoming one either."

"I hate prudish, priggish people," she said.

"What's your problem?"

She said, "What's wrong with reading French novels?"

"Did I say there was anything wrong with reading them?"

"No."

"Have you been in touch with a priest? Did he say there was anything wrong with it?"

"No."

"Any Protestants at all?"

"No. You're the only Christian I know."

I said, "How about your family?"

"I'm French! I grew up reading French novels."

"How about your mother?"

"She did, too!"

"I don't understand your problem."

She said, "Well, ever since I became a Christian, I've had the funniest guilty feeling about the books I'm reading."

"I don't know what you are reading, but take my advice and quit it." Arlette came to the Lord for the cancer, and He got into the rest of her life, including the French novels.

People always turn to Christ for something specific. There should be a *need*. Coming to Christ is not a simple "believe-ism" or a mere intellectual assent. When we preach the gospel, the fact of Jesus dying for our sins should get through to some area of people's sin.

Reaping the harvest is our responsibility. I have heard people say, "I can plow and I can plant, but reaping is the Holy Spirit's business." But so is the plowing and planting. The whole process is the Holy Spirit's business, but He uses *us* to do all three, and He *commands us* to do all three. The Holy Spirit directs us how and when to plow, plant, and reap, but the reaping remains our responsibility. If we claim it is the work of the Holy Spirit, using that as an excuse to sit around not reaping, we are abdicating a clear responsibility given to us by the Lord Himself.

Reaping should generally not be done with an ultimatum-type invitation, e.g. "Do it, or else." There *is* an "or else," but that sort of attitude can cause people to reject what they otherwise would receive.

In 1953, I gathered three Christian Navy officers in Yokosuka, Japan, and introduced them to each other.[4] We started a Bible study, but I had only a couple days there before I had to return to the States.

A year later, I got orders back to Yokosuka. I went to the Bible study my first night. There were about twenty people there. Everyone seemed to be diligently interested in the Word, except one fellow, a big, broad weight-lifter. He was sitting there flipping through the pages of a *Life* magazine while everyone else read the Scriptures.

---

4. This story is also told in my book *Weapons & Tactics* (Moscow, ID: Canon Press, 2012). A story can illustrate more than one principle.

The next day I walked into the BOQ[5] for lunch, and there he was, sitting at a table. He waved me over to eat with him. I sat down, and he said, "I'll tell you what's wrong with you Christians." I was a little taken aback, but I knew he could not possibly be talking about me, because he had only met me the night before. So I figured I would find out what was wrong with the *rest* of the Christians.

He proceeded to tell me the gospel in such a manner that it did not sound like the Word of Life at all. This is the way he heard it: "You tell a man five impossible things. First, you sit him down and tell him everybody in this world is a sinner. That's hard for me to comprehend. That is not the worst of it. Then you say that sinners go to Hell. Then you say that God somehow became a man and died for sinners! Then you say, 'He rose from the dead.' And lastly you tell him, 'If you believe it, you're saved, and if you don't believe it, you're lost.' After going through these five impossible things, the Christian says, 'Well, do you believe it?!' and the other person says, 'I don't know…' Then the Christian says, 'Well, if you believe it, you're saved, and if you don't believe it, you're lost!'"

Is that *good news?* It sounds more like bad news, doesn't it? From that moment I decided to love this man into the Kingdom so that the good news would sound like good news to him. A month later he received Christ while reading Isaiah 53.

When you give an invitation to receive Christ, do not make it sound truncated like that, even though it is true that if he doesn't believe, he is lost. He needs to know that, but when you think a person is ready to receive Christ, you want him to say *yes* to the Lord, not *no*. So do not act as if you are on one side of a rushing river and he is on the other. Do not

5. Bachelor Officer Quarters.

say, "Come across; the water's fine," when from his viewpoint it looks like the Mississippi River in the springtime—wild, turbulent, and dangerous. If you say, "Would you receive the Lord Jesus Christ?" he will say, "No." Identify with him: "Let's go through the river together. Let's call upon the Lord together."

Again, do not do this unless he is *ready*. Do not try to force a decision, or it will not be real. You need some indication that he is ripe for the harvest.

In the meantime, he may be doing everything he can to keep you from finding out that he is ripe. I was reminded of this recently when I remembered something that happened forty years ago while speaking with a physics professor. We had been talking very calmly and clearly about the gospel. Finally I gave an invitation to receive Christ. He would not. I asked him why.

He said, "I don't want to do something emotional."

"What emotion?"

I *knew* I was not causing emotion in him by how I presented the gospel. That could only mean that the gospel had gotten to him. He thought I could see it, but I could not see it until he had said that. Then I knew he really was ready. I do not remember what I said to him, but he received the Lord that night.

People try to hide their emotions when the gospel has gotten through to them. If you are alert and paying careful attention both to the Lord and to the person you are speaking to, you can see not only the emotion but also the attempts to cover it up. When I give the gospel, I talk clearly and use examples so it makes sense, being very careful not to present it in any way that would create an emotional response by my manner rather than by the gospel itself. If I suspect someone is ripe, I will ask, "Tell me, in talking to you today, have I spoken to you in an emotional manner?"

"No, no."

I say, "From my viewpoint, I've tried to make sense."

"Yes, you've made a lot of sense."

"But you're feeling emotional."

He will not say "No." He will find out that he has been caught.

"I want you to know that if I have made sense and I have not spoken in an emotional fashion, then your emotion has not been caused by the manner of my speaking. It is because there is someone else in the room, and it is not your conversation with *me* that has gotten to you. You have realized that you are in the presence of the Living God. So any decision you make from now on, pro or con, is not going to be with me. It is going to be with the Lord. I think you are ready to receive Him. If you are ready, I suggest that we pray together, and I will pray as if I were you. You can pray the prayer after me, but mean it. I'd prefer that you pray silently so you won't be tempted to talk to me. You're not talking to me. You talk to the Lord. Just so you know in advance, this is about what I would say if I were you: 'God, I'm a sinner, and I'm sick of it. I can't save myself. I believe that Jesus Christ, Your Son, died for me and rose again for me. Would You come into my life and save me and forgive me?' Shall we pray together?" Do not ask in an objective fashion; ask him in a leading way. Again, do not do this if he is not ready, because that would be unwise.

Negative emotional responses are a good indication that people are ready. People do not feel happier and happier every day until they finally say, "Boy, I'm so happy I think I'll become a Christian." It is the other way around.

Do not believe what a person tells you about himself. Listen to what he says, but if you take his words at face value, you will be led astray.

I was speaking at Goucher College years ago on "Is Christianity Credible?" Afterwards, some of the InterVarsity kids went to the counselor's home for refreshments. The InterVarsity representative came up to me and said, "Jim, we have a very intelligent girl here. She heard you tonight. She's an agnostic. You didn't make any impression on her whatsoever, but I would like you to speak to her anyhow. She's strong and intelligent, and you can't intimidate her."

I went over and, sure enough, there was this girl looking me straight in the eye, so I thought I would take the long way around—she was obviously hard ground. She needed plowing, not gospel, or so I thought. But my sense from the Holy Spirit said, "Give her your testimony with the gospel in it." I thought the Lord did not have as clear a view of the situation as I had. However, I began to give my testimony anyway. She looked at me impassively the whole time. There was no clue that anything was getting through. As I finished the testimony, I had a strong impression from the Holy Spirit to ask her to receive the Lord.

I said, "Lord, I just planted on hard ground. The seed's not even inside. It is certainly not ready." Nevertheless, I asked her to receive Jesus Christ.

She said "No."

I said, "See, Lord, I was right." But the conflict between what I was observing and what I was sensing from the Lord was so great that I knew there must be a reason for it. I said, "Lord, why is it that You've pressed me to give the gospel and this invitation? What am I not seeing?"

Then it occurred to me that in all the time I had been talking to her, she had been looking me right in the eye. When you look someone in the eye, you never look at both eyes at the same time. It is impossible. You naturally shift your gaze from one eye to the other. Yet during this whole twenty minutes, she had not shifted her gaze once. She was staring me down. She had fixed on a point at the rear of my head someplace and kept on it. Why? Because she was covering herself. She was afraid she would break if she did not. Well, I knew that was really from the Lord.

I said, "Do you know why you will not do this?"

"No. Why?"

"Because you're scared silly." Her gaze broke and she burst into tears.

I said, "Will you receive Jesus Christ?" and through all those tears, she said, "No."

Then I realized that I was standing on one side of the river and yelling at her on the other side. I backed off. "Let's call upon the Lord together," I said. She nodded her head, came to Christ, and joined InterVarsity staff that fall. Do not pay attention to what people say or what they are trying to show. Be alert to the Holy Spirit and to the person.

One last thought: when you see that someone is ready, if you have never prayed in the plowing, and never prayed in the planting, pray now. This is holy ground. The reaping is where the conflict is, where God and Satan fight the battle over an eternal soul.

Sometimes I get so afraid that I will blow it that I will just bow my head and close my eyes right in the middle of the conversation, regardless of what the other person thinks, because I want to do the right thing. Conversion is the work of the Holy Spirit. We do not want to mess it up. We are introducing people to the Eternal Father through Jesus Christ.

CHAPTER 5

An Immediate Harvest

When we first come to understand God's purposes in evangelism, we should come to see what I call the possibility of an immediate harvest. This is what I mean.

> Meanwhile His disciples urged Him, "Rabbi, eat something." But He said to them, "I have food to eat that you know nothing about." Then His disciples said to each other, "Could someone have brought Him food?" "My food," said Jesus, "is to do the will of Him who sent me and to finish His work. Do you not say, 'Four months more and then the harvest'? I tell you, open your eyes and look at the fields! They are ripe for harvest. Even now the reaper draws his wages, even now he harvests the crop for eternal life, so that the sower and reaper may be glad together. Thus the saying, 'One sows and another reaps,' is true. I sent you to reap what you have not worked for. Others have done the hard work, and you have reaped the benefits of their labor." (John 4:31-38)

In this passage Jesus speaks about reaping a harvest that someone else has planted. I suspect that when He said this

He was looking at all the people whom the Samaritan woman had gone to get streaming out of the city. They were the fields ripe for harvest.

Was this statement just true for that isolated village in the Middle East, or is it an eternal truth? If it is the latter, then there is a ripe harvest in any given society at any given instant! That might be a little too strong to argue, so let us say there is a ripe harvest in *almost* every society at *almost* any given instant. Whatever the case, *this* is a truth that does not apply only to Samaria: "I sent you to reap what you have not worked for. Others have done the hard work, and you have reaped the benefits of their labor" (John 4:38).

Matthew 9:36-38 tells us that Jesus saw the multitudes and had compassion on them because they were harassed and helpless. He said,

> The harvest is plentiful but the workers are few. Ask the Lord of the harvest, therefore, to send out workers into His harvest field. (John 9:37-38)

The *ripe* harvest is great, but there are few harvesters.

This realization struck me very strongly at one point during my service as a naval officer. I had orders for six months' temporary duty on the staff of Commander Carrier Division 5 aboard the *USS Hancock*. I did not want to go because I was with my family in Yokohama and the Lord seemed to be blessing both the family and our ministry. I did not understand how He could possibly want me out on a carrier so far away from it all. I began to pray that my orders would be canceled, but instead I found myself praying more and more that God would send me to the aircraft carrier soon.

As I prayed, I thought about this passage from Matthew. If it was true, then there would be a ripe harvest on that aircraft carrier. I would not have to plow; I would not have to plant; all I would have to say is, "Get on your knees and call upon the Lord." As I imagined what would happen aboard the carrier, I thought, "Suppose half of the officers are ready to receive Jesus Christ right now." (There were probably about 250 officers and 2,500 enlisted men on the ship.) "Suppose half of those officers are ready to receive Jesus Christ. They have had it with sin, their grandmothers have been praying for them for twenty-five years, they are remembering Sunday school verses they learned at the age of twelve, they are having problems at home, etc. Suppose during the next six months I have an opportunity to witness to half of them. Suppose I take that opportunity and leave the ship at the end of six months with *no* harvest. Great! I witnessed to the wrong half."

The idea that I could go into a situation where people wanted to know the Lord Jesus Christ and witness to everyone who was *not* ready scared me. I might plow and plant and let the ripe harvest die.

"Well," I thought, "suppose there is a ripe harvest, but only ten are ready. Could I miss ten easier than I could miss half?" I could miss ten with no difficulty at all! I was so convinced from the Lord that there was a harvest on that ship, so convinced that God wanted me there, so convinced that if left to myself I would witness to the wrong ones many times over before I reached the ready ones, that I said, "Lord, I want to *see* that ready harvest, whether it is a multitude or whether it is a few. I would like to see them brought into the kingdom if You would trust me to reach them."

However, I did not know how to recognize someone who was ready to receive Christ. I prayed that God would teach me. Then one day I was listening to a missionary someplace

(I do not remember who), and with his help I came across three instances in the New Testament that were the hardest cases of personal evangelism imaginable, and in each case the person came to Christ. They are in Acts chapters 8, 9, and 10.

The first was a case of man-to-man evangelism. I am sure you know the story, but I will tell it to you anyhow. As you read, put yourself in Philip's position. You have just been used of the Lord to bring five thousand people to Him in Colorado Springs. At the height of this great awakening you receive a message:

> Now an angel of the Lord said to Phillip, "Go south to the road—the desert road—that goes down from Jerusalem to Gaza." (Acts 8:26)

This is you. God says, "Steve, go south on the desert road from Colorado Springs to Phoenix, Arizona." Now, this angel does not even tell you if there are people on that road. You have just been used of the Lord to convert thousands, and God sends you out of this great follow-up situation into the middle of nowhere. So you go.

So he started out, and on his way he met an Ethiopian eunuch, an important official in charge of all the treasury of Candace, queen of the Ethiopians. This man had gone to Jerusalem to worship, and on his way home was sitting in his chariot reading the book of Isaiah the prophet. The Spirit told Phillip, "Go to that chariot and stay near it." Then Phillip ran up to the chariot and heard the man reading Isaiah the prophet. "Do you understand what you are reading?" Phillip asked. "How can I," he said, "unless someone explains it to me?" So he invited Phillip to come up and sit with him (Acts 8:27-31).

You are in the desert heading toward Phoenix. A limo comes along—flags on the fenders, chauffeur in the front seat, and a black man in an Armani suit in the back. The Holy Spirit says, "Go climb into the back seat with him." Just flag down the car, open the door, and hop in. Sounds easy, right?

Wrong: it was a hard case of personal evangelism. There were all kinds of problems. First, this Ethiopian was probably a Gentile. Second, eunuchs were not even allowed in the temple, according to the Old Testament. Those were two reasons a Jew would stay away from him. There are social problems, too: this man is wealthy and powerful, treasurer to a queen, and you are a hitchhiker covered in *dirt*. But the Holy Spirit said, "Go witness to him," so Phillip went. I am sure that is why God had used Philip to win all those souls in Samaria—he was obedient. He was a man who could be trusted to carry out orders. The angel gave him the command, and he went into the desert. The Holy Spirit gave him orders, and he ran toward the chariot.

This Ethiopian had gone all the way to Jerusalem to worship. He was seeking God. He had not found Him in Jerusalem, but he had found the Scriptures there, and he was coming back reading Isaiah 53:7-8. Philip asked, "Do you understand what you are reading?"

The man said, "How can I unless someone explains it to me?"

Philip began with that scriptural passage and taught him about Jesus Christ. The man believed, he was baptized at the next oasis, and they parted company.

There is a very clear principle here: *God leads the ripe harvest to the prepared harvester, and God leads the prepared harvester to the ripe harvest.* When God put those two people together, although they were different in culture, different in race, different in just about everything, there was no doubt in either person's mind what they were going to talk about. The Ethiopian was ripe; he had gone to Jerusalem seeking God. He was ready.

The second hard case is in Acts 9. A severely anti-Christian religious zealot was locking up Christians and killing them. He had cleared out Jerusalem (Acts 8:1-3) and was headed for Damascus to do the same there with authority from the chief priests.

> In Damascus there was a disciple named Ananias. The Lord called to him in a vision, "Ananias!" "Yes, Lord," he answered. The Lord told him, "Go to the house of Judas on Straight Street and ask for a man from Tarsus named Saul, for he is praying. In a vision he has seen a man named Ananias come and place his hands on him to restore his sight." "Lord," Ananias answered, "I have heard many reports about this man and all the harm he has done to Your saints in Jerusalem. And he has come here with authority from the chief priests to arrest all who call on Your name." (Acts 9:10-14)

Ananias objected to his orders: "Lord, I don't think You've got Your facts straight. You have not been reading the newspapers."

> But the Lord said to Ananias, "Go! This man is My chosen instrument to carry My name before the Gentiles and their kings and before the people of Israel. I will show him how much he must suffer for My name." Then Ananias went to the house and entered it. Placing his hands on Saul, he said, "Brother Saul, the Lord—Jesus, who appeared to you on the road as you were coming here—has sent me so that you may see again and be filled with the Holy Spirit." Immediately, something like scales fell from Saul's eyes, and he could see

again. He got up and was baptized, and after taking some food, he regained his strength. (Acts 9:15-19a)

Later Paul gave his view of this event:

I thank Christ Jesus our Lord, who has given me strength, that He considered me faithful, appointing me to His service. Even though I was once a blasphemer and a persecutor and a violent man, I was shown mercy because I acted in ignorance and unbelief. The grace of our Lord was poured out on me abundantly, along with the faith and love that are in Christ Jesus. Here is a trustworthy saying that deserves full acceptance: Christ Jesus came into the world to save sinners—of whom I am the worst. But for that very reason *I was shown mercy* so that in me, the worst of sinners, Christ Jesus might display His unlimited patience as *an example for those who would believe on Him* and receive eternal life. Now to the King eternal, immortal, invisible, the only God, be honor and glory for ever and ever. Amen (1 Tim. 1:12-17).

Notice that Paul was a blasphemer, a persecutor, a violent man, *and* ready to receive Christ. He was shown mercy for two reasons: he acted in ignorance and unbelief, and he confessed that he was the worst of sinners. Ignorance did not keep him from being the worst.

We are used to hearing of immoral sinners receiving Christ. We do not have the same hope for blaspheming, violent men. Yet God used Paul as an example of His unlimited patience for those kinds of people, that they might believe on Him and receive eternal life.

When Ananias looked at Saul of Tarsus, he saw only the outward appearance. He saw a Pharisee, a militantly, murderously anti-Christian man. Ananias thought there was no *way* that Paul was a ripe harvest. When we look on the outward appearance, what we see is the *last* kind of person we want to witness to. What we do not see is that this person has had an encounter with the Lord Jesus Christ on the way.

I do not believe Saul was converted on the road to Damascus; I believe he was converted when Ananias spoke with him and restored his sight. He was greatly *convicted* on the road, but there are several details that make it clear he was not converted there. First, he said, "Lord, what will you have me to do?" and the Lord said, "You will be told in Damascus what to do." Secondly, Paul was still blind three days later. God decided to present the message of reconciliation through a reconciled man and picked a simple disciple named Ananias. He chose someone who was *willing* to obey Him. God led Saul of Tarsus to Ananias, and God led Ananias to Saul of Tarsus. If Ananias had continued to look only on the outward appearance, God would not have been able to use him.

The third hard case of evangelism is in Acts 10. This time, the subject was a pagan officer in an imperialistic army under an emperor who claimed he was God. He was a Gentile, a foreign invader. But he was *hungry* for God and had been for a long time.

> At Caesarea there was a man named Cornelius, a centurion in what was known as the Italian Regiment. He and all his family were devout and God-fearing; he gave generously to those in need and prayed to God regularly. (Acts 10:1-2)

He was plowed and starving for seed.

> One day at about three in the afternoon he had a vision. He distinctly saw an angel of God, who came to him and said, "Cornelius!" Cornelius stared at him in fear. "What is it, Lord?" The angel answered, "Your prayers and gifts to the poor have come up as a memorial offering before God. Now

send men to Joppa to bring back a man named Simon who
is called Peter. He is staying with Simon the tanner, whose
house is by the sea." (Acts 10:3-6)

The Lord led Cornelius to Peter. He even gave him direc-
tions!

When the angel who spoke to him had gone, Cornelius
called two of his servants and a devout soldier who was one
of his attendants. He told them everything that had happened and sent them to Joppa. (Acts 10:7-8)

Meanwhile, Peter was waiting for lunch. He went up on
the rooftop, and the Lord gave him a vision. Peter did not
like the vision:

He saw the heaven opened and something like a large sheet
being let down to the earth by its four corners. It contained
all kinds of four-footed animals, as well as reptiles of the
earth and birds of the air. Then a voice told him, "Get up,
Peter. Kill and eat." "Surely not, Lord!" Peter replied. "I have
never eaten anything impure or unclean." The voice spoke to
him a second time, "Do not call anything impure that God
has made clean." This happened three times, and immediately the sheet was taken back to heaven. While Peter was
wondering about the meaning of the vision, the men sent by
Cornelius found out where Simon's house was and stopped at
the gate. They called out, asking if Simon who was known as
Peter was staying there. While Peter was still thinking about
the vision, the Spirit said to him, "Simon, three men are
looking for you. So get up and go downstairs. Do not hesitate
to go with them, for I have sent them." (Acts 10:11-20)

God very clearly brought the ripe harvest and the prepared harvester together.

One of the wonderful things about this story is that the pagan needed only one vision, but the Christian needed several. When people are ripe, they want into the kingdom far more than any Christian wants them in! This is because they are spiritually hungry, but we are spiritually satisfied and have forgotten what it is like to be without. We look at the outward appearance and say, "He's not interested." Yet the community is *crying out* for God. It was the same with Ananias; Saul wanted to see more than Ananias wanted him to.

I was thrilled with what I had learned from John 4 and Acts 8-10. I went on board the *USS Hancock* one week before Thanksgiving 1955. The first thing I did was look up my friend Ross Olson, who had just graduated from the Naval Academy and was on the *Hancock*. I unloaded all this wonderful truth from John and Acts. "Ross, this is saying that there's a ripe harvest on this ship right now. I don't know who they are, but I believe that God will lead them to us. But since we are a little dull, like Peter, I suspect He will have more success leading the harvest to us than leading us to the harvest. Let's meet here in my stateroom every afternoon at 4:30, and we'll ask God to lead the harvest to us. In the meantime, let's covenant together not to make any approaches, because we are liable to do things without the leading of the Holy Spirit." So we did.

When I came aboard, a young ensign had come with me. We were both on special duty to the Commander Carrier Division 5. I was the officer in charge. I had witnessed to this man, a Jewish officer, for months. I knew he was not ready to receive Christ. Since I was on board for the ripe harvest, I did not want to spend any more time with him until he was ripe.

We got underway, and a day later we arrived at Iwakuni in the Inland Sea. The ensign said, "Jim, let's go bicycling in the countryside on Sunday." I did not want to go because I did not want to miss the harvest, and I knew he was not it. However, I did not want to offend him, so I told him I would go, and then I prayed that it would get canceled. On Sunday morning, I got up and went topside. It was pouring pitchforks. I called his stateroom and said, "Bob, it's raining very hard." He said, "I guess we can't go bicycle riding." I hung up, praised the Lord, and went down to breakfast.

Breakfast was in the wardroom (the officers' dining room). It was a very big room because the two hundred and fifty officers normally ate there. But this was Sunday morning and we were in port, so most of them were sleeping in. I walked into the wardroom with Joe, the only Naval Academy classmate I had on the ship. I did not know him very well, since we had been in different companies at the Academy, but on our sophomore cruise to England we had been side-by-side in the same gun mount, and we were also on the same destroyer minelayer together our senior year, so I recognized him. He was the assistant landing signal officer on the *Hancock*. He would wave the planes in with a pair of paddles so they could land properly on the deck. He knew all the pilots because he had to chew them out when they made a bad landing. He was checked out in many aircraft and could do everything. He was a "tiger" in the air and a "tiger" ashore. He was the only classmate who had gotten tattooed in London on our sophomore cruise.

At breakfast together I talked the gospel to him. Later that morning at the worship service he told me that he had received Christ in his stateroom after breakfast. He was the first of the ripe harvest. He joined our prayer that God would lead the ripe harvest to us, and several other people came to the Lord without us initiating any conversations.

When he became a Christian, Joe (the landing signal officer) had said to me, "I'll live the life, but I will not witness." One day at our prayer meeting he said, "Jim, I saw a Naval Academy New Testament lying by Bill Bowen's bunk. I don't think it would be there if it weren't being read every night."

I asked him if he had talked with Bill.

"I told you I wouldn't witness to anybody."

I asked if he knew Bill.

"Well, I know him because I know all the pilots. But we don't live in the same part of the ship."

"Well, you won't witness to him, and I don't know him. It sounds like he's either a Christian or a ripe harvest, so let's ask God to lead us to Bill Bowen and Bill Bowen to us."

The very next day, the executive officer decided that everyone had to sit by rank in the wardroom. Because Joe and I were classmates, we sat next to each other. As we ate, he said, "Jim, I've got some problems in the book of Luke." We decided to go down to his stateroom and have a Bible study after supper. We were having the study when a lieutenant junior-grade walked in and asked what we were doing.

Joe said, "We're studying the Bible. Do you ever study it?"

He said, "Some."

Then Joe introduced me to Bill Bowen. In fifteen minutes he was in the kingdom.

This happened with seven or eight officers. We all held a Bible study in my stateroom seven days a week during the movie that showed in the wardroom each night. The movie was no competition for these hungry new Christians.

One day I heard from the staff that I was going to get a roommate, a public relations officer coming from the Seventh Fleet flagship. I did not want a roommate. What if he came aboard belligerent and objected to eight guys studying the Bible every night in our stateroom? I said, "Lord, I don't need a belligerent roommate. And I don't need a Christian roommate because there are so few Christians in the Pacific Fleet. You probably need him wherever he already is. But we'd be pleased if You would send us a ripe harvest." We all prayed this for several days.

I came down from work one day at four in the afternoon, and there was my new roommate. He was not tall, but he had been runner-up for Mr. California. At the age of seventeen he had been on the cover of body magazines. He had eighteen-inch biceps. He had also carried a first-string lineman position (offense and defense) for three years on the Naval Academy football team while weighing only 180 pounds.

There he was, shirt off, muscles rippling everywhere—all I could see was one big wedge of muscle. He was not smiling, and as I looked at him I thought, "Lord, You sent the wrong man." I was *convinced* this was not the one we asked for. What was I going to do? If I told him about the Lord or even about the Bible study, he was liable to pick me up and wipe me around the room. I was really scared. (As it turns out, he was also scared because I outranked him.) I knew I had to tell him that in a few hours naval officers were going to come into the room for a Bible study. I could not cancel it: the officers lived all over the ship, and I did not know how to get word to all of them.

I began to tell my new roommate about the study in an apologetic fashion, and he listened without saying anything. I told him *why* we studied the Bible, and he kept listening. I told him how I had come to know Jesus Christ. I just kept talking and talking. I was scared to quit because I was afraid he would *say* something. I went through my whole testimony and the gospel before I quit.

When I finally finished, he said, "Jim, do you know what I said when I came into the room this afternoon?"

"What?"

"At last, a Bible." He had been looking for spiritual answers for months. He read the gospel of John that night and all of Matthew the next night. Sometimes he stayed for the Bible studies; sometimes he did not. On Christmas Eve, 1955, just about a month after I had come aboard, he was in the Bible study, and Joe said, "Alex, why don't you become a Christian?"

"I don't know, Joe, why should I?"

So Joe told him. I was amazed, because Joe had said he would never witness to anyone.

Alex said, "Okay, Joe. What do I have to do?"

Joe turned him over to me, and Alex called upon the Lord Jesus Christ. In 1959 he got out of the Navy and entered Fuller Seminary, then came back to the Navy in 1965 as a chaplain for Destroyer Squadron Eight.

I left the *Hancock* in two months instead of six. In the two months I was aboard, about ten officers and thirty-five enlisted men came to Christ, and I did not initiate the message with any of them. A friend told me that this pattern continued after I left the ship. God will wonderfully guide you to the ripe people. More importantly, He will guide them to you.

A few years later, I was in Washington, DC, headed for Pittsburgh. In those days people lined up to get on planes; there were no assigned seats. The plane was late getting loaded, and I happened to be the first in line. The fellow behind me was a real estate agent; he liked to talk, and he was talking, but I was not encouraging him. I said, "Lord, I don't want to miss the right one by getting sidetracked by this guy." So I ignored him. But then I prayed and said, "Lord, if you want me to witness to this fellow, have him sit next to me when I get on the airplane." Since I would be the first one on, the rest of the plane would be empty when he boarded. The chances of him sitting next to me were pretty slim. It is an unwritten rule: you sit with someone you do not know only after all the window seats are full. I sat down, and he sat beside me. I thanked God.

I do not remember how the conversation started. When someone is ripe, you do not have to figure out how to start; it is just obvious. He accepted the Lord. After he had received the Lord, he said, "Boy, this is the greatest coincidence of my life. I've been an atheist for years. But a month ago I started going to church, and a week ago I started reading the Bible, and now I meet you on this airplane! I've never run into such a coincidence in my life!"

I said, "It wasn't a coincidence. I asked the Lord to let me sit with you."

The biggest problem we have in witnessing is that God cannot trust Christians because Christians do not trust Him. People want in the kingdom much more than we want them in. Think of this: how many people in this world did Jesus Christ die for? Everybody! How many is He willing should perish?

> This is good, and pleases *God our Savior, who wants all men to be saved* and to come to a knowledge of the truth (1 Tim. 2:3-4).

How many people did He send us to? Everybody. He died for everyone, not willing that any should perish. Why isn't there a great influx into the kingdom? I would suggest that it is because Christians don't want it. God has limited Himself to presenting the message of reconciliation through reconciled men. He could have given the gospel to Cornelius by that angel. He could have done the same with the Ethiopian. He could have done the same with Saul of Tarsus. He had access to all of them Himself. Yet He chose to give the message through reconciled men.

There is no great influx into the kingdom because Christians are not ready and willing to recognize the harvest. If you cannot trust yourself to find it, ask God to lead the harvest to you. He will lead someone, and you may miss him because you are not in the habit of recognizing a harvest. Ask the Lord to send him by again, or go chase him. God uses people who are willing to be used.

Twenty years later a young couple came into Crossroads bookstore in Moscow, Idaho. It became obvious to me that the girl was a Christian from the happiness and excitement she expressed when she saw books she recognized. She continued looking for at least thirty minutes while the young man stood by. When they were ready to pay for her books, I asked them if they were active in any student group on campus. He replied that they were looking for a church they could attend together. Her background was Baptist; his was Unitarian and Presbyterian. I recommended three strong Christian churches in the area, which they appreciated. Then I asked them what their real interest was, i.e., apart from the denominations, what did they believe about Jesus Christ?

"I'm ready to be convinced," he said.

"Ready enough to read a book?"

"Yes."

I went to the shelf and picked up *Basic Christianity* by John R.W. Stott, which he purchased.

Then I asked him if he was ready enough to talk to someone, and again he replied that he was. I spent the next forty-five minutes with him in my office teaching and making clear to him the good news of Jesus Christ. There was no argument, and he had no questions. As he had said, he was ready. He must have received Christ shortly after leaving the store because when he came in the next time, he was a Christian.

> Open your eyes and look at the fields! They are ripe for harvest. (John 4:35b)

CHAPTER 6

TO WIN AS MANY
AS POSSIBLE

What is the goal of our evangelism?

Though I am free and belong to no man, *I make myself a slave to everyone to win as many as possible.* To the Jews I became like a Jew to win the Jews. To those under the law I became like one under the law, though I myself am not under the law, so as to win those under the law. To those not having the law I became like one not having the law, though I am not free from God's law but am under Christ's law, so as to win those not having the law. To the weak I became weak to win the weak. I have become all things to all men so that by all possible means I might save some. I do this for the sake of the gospel, that I may share in its blessings. (1 Cor. 9:19-23)

Paul was in *voluntary* servitude to *everyone.* This is not a new idea, but it is new to our thinking. How many people today make themselves slaves to other people to win them for Christ? Not many. Nor do people who speak on evangelism often teach it.

Paul does not say that he makes himself a slave to everyone to win *everyone*, but to win *as many as possible*. Therefore, if I do not make myself a slave to everyone, I am limiting the possibility of how many will be saved.

How in the world can you be a slave to everyone? Paul breaks it down in verse 20: "To the Jews I became like a Jew." Why? To win the Jews. If Christians want to win Mormons today, do they become like Mormons? No. If they want to win Muslims, do they become like Muslims? Not usually. Overseas, on the mission field, they are more likely to do this, because they know they need to learn the language and the culture of the people. However, we need to learn the language and culture *wherever we are*, without compromising on the basics of the Christian faith.

Almost every society is involved in some form of paganism or idolatry. How do you learn the culture and not get mixed up in the idolatry and the religious beliefs? Paul managed it with the Jews: "To those under the law I became like one under the law." He added, "Though I myself am not under the law." Paul was not under the law, but he became *like* one under the law, but without compromising. Paul *identified* with the people culturally without actually getting back under the legalism of the Old Testament. He could not become *truly* like the Jews because he was no longer under the law, but under grace.

On the other hand, we say we are going to obey God's law, and we are not about to get close to anyone who is living in licentiousness. We will win them from a distance, shouting at them over the radio . . . if they tune in. Yet Paul says, "Why do I become as one not under the law? So as to win those not having the law."

"To the weak I became weak." People spend their whole lives trying to keep from being weak. We do not *want* to identify with the weak. We even take self-improvement courses to make ourselves stronger. Paul repeats what he said at the beginning: "I have become *all* things to *all* men, so that by all possible means I might save some."

I have never seen any teaching on evangelism that says this is the way to do it. We have many other methods, but not voluntary servitude to the person you want to win. We think, "If I were the master, then I could win my slaves." Christian humility says with Paul, "If I were the *slave*, I could win the master." Jesus Himself told us, "He who would be first among you, let him be servant of all" (Mark 9:35). Humility reflects Jesus Christ much more than authority does.

There is a Christian magazine called *Leadership*. Do we have one called *Slavery*? It is voluntary slavery that brings people to Christ, not leadership. This is what Jesus taught us: "As I have washed your feet, you ought to wash one another's feet" (John 13:14). That is a humbling thing to do, and the Bible says it is good. When we avoid humbling ourselves because we do not like it, fewer people are saved. The Apostle Paul was determined that if there was any limitation in people's salvation, it would not be because of his witness. "I am innocent of the blood of all men," he declared (Acts 20:26). He was referring to this passage in Ezekiel:

> When I say to the wicked man, "You shall surely die," and you do not warn that wicked man to turn from his wicked ways, he will die in his iniquity. But his blood I will require at your hand (Ezek. 3:18).

Most people are culturally rigid. If someone is of a different background, if they are lower-class financially, lower-class educationally, higher-class financially, higher-class socially, of a different race, etc., we do not know how to identify with them. We feel uncomfortable around them, and we also do not know how to make them feel comfortable. But everyone around us should know that we love them, and not just because we *say* we do.

I became a Christian in 1947 during my second year at the Naval Academy. I had three years there as a Christian, then I went six years in the Pacific Fleet and afterwards went back to work with cadets and midshipmen until 1968. This meant that for twenty-one years my only contact was with people with short hair. Then I moved to Ann Arbor, Michigan, in 1968. That was the wrong place to be looking for short hair.

I had identified with the midshipmen. I was used to the Navy culture. I had become like a midshipman to reach midshipmen. I had become like the naval officers to reach the naval officers. However, I was unwilling to identify with people in other cultures, and I did not realize that while I was working with naval officers. I only found out I was not when I started running into people from other backgrounds.

That was when I was still in Annapolis, in '58 or '59. I opened a bookstore on Maryland Avenue near the main gate of the Naval Academy in order to reach the midshipmen. The problem was that little old ladies would come in wanting Bible storybooks for their grandchildren. I did not want to waste my time showing children's books to grandmothers! I was *focused*! Many, many kinds of people came into the store. In fact, everyone came in *except* the midshipmen, because they were required to stay on base at the Naval Academy.

One of our regular customers was a janitor at Bancroft Hall[6] who was also an orderly at the hospital. There were several things that made it hard for me to relate to him: 1) he was black, 2) he was a custodian, and 3) he was Roman Catholic. One day he said, "Mr. Wilson, I understand you start Bible studies. I've got four or five guys who want to know how to study the Bible. Would you teach us?"

I couldn't say no to that, regardless what my cultural rigidity was. I told him I would meet with them once or twice to help them get started. I sat down with him and gave him some instructions on how to do inductive Bible studies, but I saw he was not paying any attention. I did not know what to do. I was uncomfortable.

He said, "Mr. Wilson, do you know why I want to study the Bible?"

I said, "No."

"We all want to know how to be born again." He became a Christian then and there.

I had only wanted to reach midshipmen. This man reached several barbers and Bancroft Hall custodians for the Lord. He also bought dozens of intellectual books and commentaries from our store to keep at Bancroft Hall and the hospital. Over time he accumulated one of the biggest libraries in Annapolis, and he had read every book in it. Through him the midshipmen I had wanted to reach started coming to the Lord—because they all had to sit in barber chairs.

When you close your heart to one section of the population, you also close your heart to the section of the population that you want to reach. By closing your heart to other cultures, you become

6. The dormitory at the Naval Academy, which housed four thousand midshipmen.

less effective in the culture you are already in. You need to be wide open to everyone.

Once when I was at graduate school in Monterey, California, I had to go to the Navy dentist. The dentist was not there, but the technician, an enlisted man, was. As he was cleaning my teeth, I started talking to him about God. He was so interested he said, "Come with me into the x-ray room." I went into the developing room with him and kept talking to him about the Lord. Every time I went to the dentist, I would talk to this fellow about God—but I talked to him the way an officer talks to an enlisted man. In the Navy they teach the officers not to have social relationships with enlisted men, and I was acting according to that protocol.

One day I got a phone call from him. "Mr. Wilson, I've got orders to Kodiak, Alaska. Could my wife and I come over and see you?"

I was not supposed to give hospitality to enlisted men. I found myself caught between my Christianity and my Navy culture. I said, "Sure, come on over."

When he arrived, I did not know what to do with him. We sat there awkwardly, and I started talking about the weather. He was twenty-one years old, his wife was about eighteen, and they had a little baby with them. After a while his wife said, "Mr. Wilson, my husband tells me you talk about God." He had told her everything I had said at the dentist's office.

I said, "Yes." Still feeling awkward, I started in Genesis and headed toward Revelation, telling them about God. Soon I saw they were not paying attention.

Finally the Holy Spirit said: "Wilson, shut up and let these people get saved!" I stopped what I was saying and asked them, "Would you like to become Christians?"

They looked at each other, jumped off the couch, and got on their knees. They even put the baby on the floor. Bessie came in, scooped up the baby, and took it to the kitchen. They were converted. They were *ready* to be converted when they called me on the telephone, and I wasted time talking about the weather and theology because I had not related to them.

When I moved to Ann Arbor, Michigan, I found that the culture there was radically different from Navy-influenced Annapolis. There were long-haired University of Michigan students, SDS members,[7] Black Panthers, all kinds of people. Was I going to grow out my hair, have a beard, wear chains? I made the decision that *I was willing to.* Then I realized that a lot of other people were doing those things, but it was only a *surface* identification; it was not a *heart* identification. It dawned on me that if I had a heart identification, I did not need the surface one. People see through the phonies very quickly. If you love people from the heart, you do not have to change clothes every time you go to a different group. You can be a slave to everyone in your *heart.* Even now I still feel rigid sometimes just because of my cultural background and education, but I find that people do not feel rigid with me. I think it is because I made that choice to identify with them in my heart.

Aren't we called to be holy and separated from the world, to *appear* different so that people know that we believe and adhere to the commands of Scripture? Yes. We *are* called to be separate from the world. That is why Paul identified with people without compromising. Those under the law were legally moral, separatists in a sense. Those who were

7. Students for a Democratic Society, a radical student group of the sixties.

not under the law were probably licentious. But Paul said he was still under the law to Christ. *He never compromised on real obedience to God.* The problem with the church today (and probably with the church then) is that it tends to make "commands of God" that are not in the Scripture. Jesus said He wants us to be in the world, but not of the world. Our problem is we are trying not to be *in* it. If we allow people see our vulnerability, our love, our identification with them, they will want what we have. Think of Peter's vision as he described it in Acts 11:

> The apostles and the brothers throughout Judea heard that the Gentiles also had received the word of God. So when Peter went up to Jerusalem, the circumcised believers criticized him and said, "You went into the house of uncircumcised men and ate with them." Peter began and explained everything to them precisely as it had happened: "I was in the city of Joppa praying, and in a trance I saw a vision. I saw something like a large sheet being let down from heaven by its four corners, and it came down to where I was. I looked into it and saw four-footed animals of the earth, wild beasts, reptiles, and birds of the air. Then I heard a voice telling me, 'Get up, Peter. Kill and eat.' I replied, 'Surely not, Lord! Nothing impure or unclean has ever entered my mouth.' The voice spoke from heaven a second time, 'Do not call anything impure that God has made clean.' This happened three times, and then it was all pulled up to heaven again. Right then three men who had been sent to me from Caesarea stopped at the house where I was staying. The Spirit told me to have no hesitation about going with them. These six brothers also went with me, and we entered the man's house. He told us how he had seen an angel appear in his house and say, 'Send to Joppa for Simon who is called Peter. He will bring you a message through which you and all your household will be saved.' As I began to speak, the Holy Spirit came on them as he had come on us at the beginning. Then

I remembered what the Lord had said: 'John baptized with water, but you will be baptized with the Holy Spirit.' So if God gave them the same gift as he gave us, who believed in the Lord Jesus Christ, who was I to think that I could oppose God?" When they heard this, they had no further objections and praised God, saying, "So then, God has granted even the Gentiles repentance unto life." (Acts 11:1-18)

"Come out from among them and be ye separate" and "Touch not the unclean thing" are biblical commands, but we have defined the unclean things differently from how the Bible defines them. That difference keeps us out of effective evangelism.

My wife's background was Prairie Bible Institute, a little Bible college in Three Hills, Alberta, Canada, that probably puts out more missionaries per square foot than any other school in the world. When it came to separation from the world, Prairie did it in spades. While Bessie was there, the boys sat on one side of the dining room and the girls sat on the other side. The girls had to have long sleeves, regardless what the style was, and skirts that were no more than eleven inches from the floor. One time, they came in, and the boys had pasted a poster on the girls' side of the room. It read, "The Promised Land."

As a result of our backgrounds, Bessie and I together could sign the longest list of "Don'ts" in any fundamentalist church in the country if we wanted to. But we would not do it. We would not join a church that required it because of the biblical requirement to be a servant to all. We found that we could reach people without conforming either to the world or the fundamentalist churches.

Maybe when you were growing up you wondered why older ladies always wore bright red lipstick. The reason is that is what they wore when they were sixteen! Bessie was in that age group. She never wore any herself, but that did not stop her from reaching people when everyone else was wearing a lot of makeup. Then came the '60s and '70s when nobody wore lipstick, or at least none of the young people did, and Bessie was right with them. I am sure they thought she had identified with them because all the other older women wore it. We are all inflexible to some extent. But we *don't* have to be inflexible heart-wise. If you cannot be flexible in your dress, be flexible inside, because it means the salvation of the world.

One time in Annapolis, I picked up a hitchhiker. He was black, a very friendly guy, and very thankful. He was on his way back to work after going to the motor vehicle place to get his driver's license. I asked him what year he graduated from Annapolis High.

He said, "'78."

"Oh. Did you go to Adams Park Elementary?"

He said, "Yeah! I went to Adams Park."

Heather (our daughter) and Gordon (our youngest son) had been at Adams Park at the same time he would have been there. We had identified. We had a very warm, very friendly conversation; I knew he did not sense any difference between us.

"How do I do this?" you might ask. "I don't want to pick up any hitchhikers." Stretch yourself. Before you do, pray and choose to love the person you've never met, whoever it is.

When he was a pastor in New England, my brother said to me once, "Jim, I'm a Christian. I'm supposed to love people all over the world. There are millions of people in Africa. I cannot even picture millions of people. How do I love them all when I don't even know them?"

Love does not depend on knowing them. It depends upon the infinite amount of love that *God* has for you and through you. *Choose* to love the millions of people in Africa so that if any one of them shows up in your office, he can tell immediately that you really love him, because you previously made the decision to love him. It has nothing to do with what he is. People know right from the start whether you love them or not, and you do not have to be gushy to prove it. You do not have to *say* you love them. They will pick up on it if you really do love them. This was the choice that Paul made: "I make myself a slave to everyone." It was not conditional. He did not stop to see what that "everyone" looked like.

Loving the complete stranger is central to the gospel:

> The alien living with you must be treated as one of your native-born. Love him as yourself, for you were aliens in Egypt. I am the LORD your God. (Lev. 19:34)

The "alien" is someone from a different culture, someone not like us. The Bible says we are to have the same love for him as for people from our own culture. One pastor put it this way:

> All men are strangers to God, being born far away from Him and cut off in their sins. God treats strangers with grace, mercy, and longsuffering, and expects His people to do the same, thus revealing Himself in their daily actions.[8]

This is not a mechanical formula. It is not a list of things to say or verses to memorize. It is a basic principle of Christianity. Jesus Christ died for all men. His death was the greatest expression of love in the history of the world, and we are the bearers of that Message. If the messengers do not have the

8. Steve Wilkins, *Face to Face* (Moscow, ID: Canon Press, 2010), 107.

love that they are declaring, the message is a dead one. If we give the message in a sterile fashion, we cannot say, "They got the message. Their blood is not on my hands." No. Confess that you do not love them and choose to love them, by God's grace. You have to choose it. If you are waiting for the love to hit you, you are in *trouble*. There is no way you are going to fall in love with your enemy. *Choose* to make yourself a slave to everyone. Choose to be available at their request.

> So whether you eat or drink, or whatever you do, do it all for the glory of God. Do not cause anyone to stumble, whether Jews, Greeks, or the church of God. (1 Cor. 10:31-32)

This is an evangelistic passage. Paul was not just referring to the brothers. This includes Jews (people who were not Christians), Greeks (people who were not Christians), and the church of God (Christians). Verse 32: *Do not cause anyone to stumble.* This is a command, not a suggestion. Verse 33 is an example:

> …even as I try to please everyone in every way. For I am not seeking my own good but the good of many, so that they may be saved. (1 Cor. 10:33)

"You can't please everybody" is a standard American idiom. It implies, "So don't bother to try." Yet Paul says he tries to please everybody. What he means is that he is not trying to please *himself.* "For I am not seeking my own good, but the good of many, *so that they may be saved.*"

What are we to do?

> Follow my example as I follow the example of Christ. (1 Cor. 11:1)

This is *not* optional. It is a command. We all hold to the authority of the scriptures in our heads, but when it comes to obeying it, we fudge. The liberals are at least honest about it: they say the Bible is not true. We say it *is* true, but we are not willing to obey it.

Perhaps we can imagine being a slave to a few people. We can also imagine how they might react—tromp all over us, hurt us. In 1 Peter 2, Peter gives these instructions to slaves:

> Slaves, submit yourselves to your masters with all respect, not only to those who are good and considerate, but also to those who are harsh. For it is commendable if a man bears up under the pain of unjust suffering because he is conscious of God. But how is it to your credit if you receive a beating for doing wrong and endure it? But if you suffer for doing good, and you endure it, this is commendable before God. (1 Pet. 2:18-20)

Peter wrote this to people who were involuntarily enslaved. He told them to submit with all respect, not because their masters were respectable, and even if they were not.

> To this you were called because Christ suffered for you, leaving you an example that you should follow in His steps. He committed no sin; no deceit was found in His mouth; when they hurled the insults at Him, He did not retaliate; when He suffered, He made no threats. Instead, He entrusted Himself to Him who judges justly. (1 Pet. 2:21-23)

Christ is our example. When they tromped all over Him, He did not retaliate.

I want to use a word that people do not like. It is the word "vulnerable." Did Christ make Himself vulnerable? Yes. Did He tell us that we should be vulnerable? Yes. We think that if we make ourselves vulnerable, we will be taken advantage of all over the place. It is a possibility. It certainly happened to Jesus. But that is *not* a reason to disobey.

This kind of vulnerability is the way Jesus Christ won people—through His death on the cross. We want to build a hedge around ourselves so we will not get hurt. Jesus teaches that we are to put ourselves in a position where we might get hurt. It wins people.

You may fear being taken advantage of. That is normal. Nobody wants to get walked on. *Nobody* wants to be stomped, even very strong people. In general, everyone would rather do the walking than the getting walked on. No one is *naturally* willing to be a slave to someone else because that means the other person is in control and can do what he wants, and it might not be nice. Yet who really wins when we make ourselves vulnerable to the lost? *We do*, and they get won to Christ.

CHAPTER 7

DO NOT RESIST AN EVIL PERSON

What do we do with the really hard passages?

You have heard that it was said, "Eye for eye, and tooth for tooth." But I tell you, do not resist an evil person. If anyone slaps you on the right cheek, turn to them the other cheek also. And if anyone wants to sue you and take your shirt, hand over your coat as well. If anyone forces you to go one mile, go with them two miles. Give to the one who asks you, and do not turn away from the one who wants to borrow from you. (Matt. 5:38-42)

Do not resist an evil person. This is certainly not natural and not what we want to do, either. It is a very hard passage.

The text does not say why to not resist an evil person. People do not like that. They want a reason before they are willing to obey, so I will give one: evangelism.

This is how you win evil people. Although Jesus does not say that explicitly, it becomes clear if you imagine doing the opposite: someone sues you for your cloak, and you counter-sue him. Will you win him to Christ that way? A man hits you on your right cheek, so you hit him. He asks to borrow from you, and you say, "No way. Go to the bank." Doing what we *feel* like doing in that kind of situation is not effective evangelism, and we know it.

"That's right," you might think, "but this guy is an evil person. Why does it matter?" It matters because Jesus Christ did not die for *nice* people. He did not die, as we often are tempted to think, for the ones that are not *too* bad. In this passage, Christ assumed that the other guy was evil—*maliciously* evil. When I teach on this, people often tell me, "But this guy is evil. He's ripping me off!" That is exactly what Jesus was talking about. Shouldn't we be glad we found a situation that fits so exactly?

> *Bless those who persecute you;* bless and do not curse. Rejoice with those who rejoice; mourn with those who mourn. Live in harmony with one another. Do not be proud, but be willing to associate with people of low position. Do not be conceited. Do not repay anyone evil for evil. Be careful to do what is right in the eyes of everybody. If it is possible, as far as it depends on you, live at peace with everyone. Do not take revenge, my friends, but leave room for God's wrath, for it is written: "It is mine to avenge; I will repay," says the Lord. On the contrary: "If your enemy is hungry, feed him; if he is thirsty, give him something to drink. In doing this, you will heap burning coals on his head." Do not be overcome by evil, but overcome evil with good." (Rom. 12:14-21)

We are to permit people to walk all over us. This is the opposite of what the world and even many Christians teach. But it is effective evangelism.[9]

9. Heaping coals of fire on the head of your enemy is part of this effective evangelism. My son Douglas, also a pastor, explains the verse this way: "The question of what those 'coals of fire' are has been much

What about when other people are getting walked on? If I am strolling down the street and someone hits me, I should turn the other cheek, not only physically, but also in my heart. I want to reach that person for Christ. But if I am walking down the street and someone knocks my wife over, I do not pick her up and turn her around so he can hit *her* other cheek. Do not help *someone* else turn the other cheek. In a situation like that I am a representative of God, the state, and my family and am required to restrain the evil person and help the one who is being attacked. We are biblically responsible for protecting *other people* from evil.

I want to make one last clarification concerning not resisting an evil person. There are people who are what you might call "doormats." I am not talking about that. Doormats allow themselves to be walked all over, too. However, they are not in control. When Jesus Christ submitted, *He* did so in such a way as that He was running the show. When Paul was in chains, *he* was the boss, although he was a boss in a submissive way. Biblical submission to evil people is a position of *strength*, not weakness.

Beware of making exceptions to the rule of turning the other cheek. There may be legitimate ones, but once people start making exceptions, they keep on making them, and soon they are not turning the other cheek at all. But sure-

---

discussed. Is this a kind act, a helping hand that puts starter coals in somebody's basin that they carry home on their head? That has the feel of a Bible handbook answer. Are these coals of fire an image of judgment (Ps. 18:12-13)? Or perhaps conviction of sin? That is possible, but given what is said about overcoming evil in the next verse, I would take it as an act of consecration. Treat your enemy like he was an altar (Lev. 16:12)." [Douglas Wilson, "Coals of Fire on the Head," Blog and Mablog, http://dougwils.com/s8-expository/coals-of-fire-on-the-head.html (accessed 2/20/2014).] This is loving your enemy into the kingdom; your work of giving him food and drink is helping to set him aside for God.

ly the verse means *something*. Rather than thinking of the money involved or the evil or the incompetence, think of evangelism. Do you win the person who is sinning against you *any other way* than turning the other cheek? No. Of course, you might not win him this way, but you will almost certainly *lose* him the other way!

CHAPTER 8

FOUR WILLS OF CONVERSION

One of the more obvious things about evangelism is the fact that it involves quite a number of persons.

And the Lord's servant must not quarrel; instead, he must be kind to everyone, able to teach, not resentful. Those who oppose him he must gently instruct, in the hope that God will grant them repentance leading them to a knowledge of the truth, and that they will come to their senses and escape from the trap of the devil, who has taken them captive to do his will. (2 Tim. 2:24-26)

There are four wills involved in conversion: *God's, the devil's, the sinner's, and the Christian's.*

The key will in salvation is the Lord's. He came to earth in the middle of history and paid the sin penalty for all men. He accomplished redemption. He finished His work so that by His active obedience and His sacrifice for sin all men everywhere could know the Savior.

The second most important will is not the non-Christian's will. It is the Christian's. It is to the Christian that

Paul speaks in 2 Timothy. He says that Satan and the non-Christian react to God's will *and to the manner in which the Christian presents it.* A Christian's obedience to God in his expression of God's will for the non-Christian determines how the non-Christian will respond.

What is God's will for non-Christians? It is the gospel. How are we to present it? Ephesians 4 talks of "speaking the truth in love." Love is vital in the presentation of the gospel. Earlier I mentioned an example of the truth expressed in an unloving fashion by the man I met in the Yokosuka BOQ. That Navy officer made the good news sound like bad news. Speaking the truth alone is not good enough. The truth can condemn; so you must speak the truth *in love.*

Early in my Christian life, I felt the need for an adequate apologetic for every question to and accusation against the Christian faith. There were so many people who did not know God, and there were so many questions that seemed to stand between them and Him. I thought that if I could answer their questions clearly, rationally, and kindly, they would be convinced and would become believers. So I set myself the task of acquiring the right answers.

Before I had gotten very far in this pursuit, I began to have doubts. I was practicing my growing knowledge in face-to-face encounters and large bull sessions. It was great fun arguing; it was even more fun winning the argument. But there were not any results. Part of the problem was that I found it difficult to be kind while I was being methodical and following clear lines of rational argument in my presentations. Then I noticed something else—most of the people with the questions did not really want answers. They just wanted to have questions.

Foolish and unlearned questions avoid. Have nothing to do with stupid, senseless controversies, knowing that they bring quarrels, knowing that they do gender strife. (2 Tim. 2:23, KJV)

When you answer foolish and unlearned question, it leads to arguments. Paul says that the servant of the Lord must not strive. He must not. That does not mean compromising his position; it means that he does not talk to people about stupid, senseless questions.

Not everyone who asks a question really wants an answer. In most cases, they are just looking for a fight. If you end up giving someone a fight because you thought he wanted answers, you have disobeyed the Scriptures. You are a servant of the Lord. You must not strive. You must not quarrel. God told us to be *kind* to everyone. You cannot quarrel kindly. "And the Lord's servant must…be kind to everyone, *able to teach, not resentful.* Those who oppose him he must *gently instruct…*" We are to be able teachers, kind and gentle. God may grant repentance to those we witness to when we avoid quarreling and are kind. Then people will escape from the snare of the devil. Right now they are caught in his man trap. When the Christian teaches the gospel kindly and gently, it causes repentance. God springs the trap, and people escape from the grasp of the devil.

The non-Christian's will only comes into play once the trap has been opened. Up to that point, he has been held captive to the devil's will. The Lord Jesus Christ died to destroy the power of death, that is, the devil, and to deliver those who through fear of death were all their lifetime subject to bondage. The one power is in the cross, and the other power is in the devil, but what makes the power of the cross active is the way the Christian presents the gospel.

How do you know if a question is foolish and unlearned? There are several ways to tell. First, is a fool asking it? The Scripture says, "The fool has said in his heart there is no God" (Psalm 53:1). If a person asks you to prove the existence of God, he probably does not want to listen to the proof.

Second, there is a certain kind of question that people do not usually want real answers to, even though you might know them. These are questions like: "Where did Cain get his wife?" "What about the innocent man in Africa?" (Even though that last one sounds like a legitimate question, it is hypothetical. There are no innocent men in Africa...or anyplace else, for that matter.) Do not let the other person assume the center. Do not respond on his terms. He is just looking for a fight.

You can also tell whether someone wants an answer by *how* he asks the question. Sometimes a question might be perfectly legitimate in itself, but the questioner's manner indicates that he does not really want an answer.

Lastly, look back to all the quarrels you have been in with non-Christians. Tabulate the questions that got you into those quarrels.

Do not quarrel. At the same time, *do not* compromise. Paul says to *instruct* your opponents with *gentleness*. You are still doing the instructing.

Instead, avoid the question. In this culture, we tend to think that if someone asks a question, we are obligated to answer it. We are *not* obligated. How many questions did Jesus answer? Not many. He kept command of the conversation. He talked on *His* terms. He *was* asked questions, but He either avoided them, turned them around, or directed some other statement to the situation so that He was always talking on *His* conditions. We are told to do the same. "But they'll think bad thoughts of us if we avoid the question. They'll think we don't know the answer." Well, that is alright. That is better than starting a quarrel.

One way to avoid a foolish question is to ask the person if he really wants to know the answer. If he says, "No, I guess I didn't really want to know," then you say, "Well, then why did you ask it?"

Suppose he says, "Yes."

Then you say, "Do you believe I know the answer?"

"No."

"Then why did you ask me?"

Or he says, "Yes, I think you know the answer."

"Are you prepared to receive it?"

"No, I'm not really sure I am."

"Well, then I am not prepared to answer it."

There are other ways to avoid the question. You can always say that you don't know the answer. Or you can say, "I know the answer, but I'm not going to tell you." Do not say this belligerently; just say it positively, letting them know that you are sure of your position.

When these ideas will not work, simply pray for wisdom on how to avoid the question. You do not have to answer it.

Sometimes people set up a slew of conditions they want you to meet before they will become Christians. They say they will believe if someone just answered their questions about Christianity. But often they have no intention of letting anyone do that, because they are not prepared to receive the answers. After you get done answering, they say, "Well, that's not my real problem…"

After I graduated from the Naval Academy, I went home to small town Nebraska. My parents had moved to that town after I left home for the Naval Academy, so I did not know very many people. The day I arrived, two of my brothers and two of their friends became Christians. Two days later there was a father-son banquet at the Methodist Church, and because my father had six sons, we all went.

I walked home alone that evening. In the rural Midwest, the driveway and the yard are the same thing: cars drive into the front yard and turn around. As I was walking up to our house, I noticed a car parked in the yard. I did not recognize it, and I did not know anyone was in it.

Then a voice called out from the car. "Jim, we've got some questions about religion." Well, I knew what they would be—stupid, foolish questions—and that I would be talking all night. I did not know who had asked the question, but I knew the four converts from two days earlier had shaken up the town.

I said to the voice, "Well, I've got lots of answers, but I'm not giving any. Good night."

There was silence at the other end. I took two more steps; then I turned around and said, "I'll tell you what. I'll answer one question. I pick it."

The voice came back, "What's the question?"

"If you'd like to know how to become a Christian, I'll tell you. If not, I'm going to bed."

There was a long pause. Then finally he said, "That's what we'd really like to know."

If I had let them pick the questions, we would never have gotten around to that one. I climbed in the back seat and went through the gospel, and three eighteen-year-old boys put their trust in the Savior. The one in the middle was my brother who had been kicking things around the house for two days because his older brother and his younger brother had both received Christ, and he was greatly convicted.

If you hold off the questions, you reach the real problem sooner. People say that they will become Christians if you answer their objections, but very seldom is this actually true. Why? *Because the problem of salvation is a moral one, not an intellectual one.* His real issue is that he does not want to turn from sin. The questions are just roadblocks.

Years ago, in Montgomery, Alabama, I was talking with an Air Force officer who said, "Jim, Christianity seems so impossible; but if I could believe all this was true—intellectually true—I'd become a Christian right now."

I said, "No, you wouldn't."

"Yes, I would! Everlasting life? Forgiveness of sins? Love, joy, peace? If it were truth, I'd be foolish not to want those things. My only problem is that these intellectual questions come between me and belief."

I started to answer some of his questions. Ordinarily I would not do this; I give books to people who really want answers. But this time I talked, and three hours later he said, "Jim, I didn't think this would ever happen, but I'm convinced. You've really answered all of my problems with Christianity!"

I said, "Of course you'll get on your knees right now and call on the Lord Jesus Christ."

"Wait a minute!"

"What do you mean, 'Wait a minute'? You said three hours ago you would become a Christian right away if your problems were answered, and you just told me they were answered!"

"I know, I know. But wait a minute."

"I said that you wouldn't become a Christian. The real trouble is not your intellectual problems at all, but your sin."

Christ died for sinners, not for intellectual doubters. A lot of people hide behind academic questions to avoid the real issue. The only common denominator in this world is sin. Men love their sin. I am not saying that answers given in an apologetic fashion can never be helpful, but *they do not cause people to become Christians.* Answering intellectual questions might open the door a little bit and highlight the real problem, but it is the gospel and repentance from sin that brings people to Christ.[10]

In 1957, I was on a trip to Boston on business for the Officers' Christian Union. John Stott was conducting a mission at Harvard,[11] so I called the InterVarsity office at Harvard to ask if they could use any help. It turned out that they were short an assistant missioner for Dunster House, one of the Harvard houses. The object of the assistant missioner was to go into the house and get into a bull session with all the undergraduates to fire them up so they would go hear John Stott in the evening.

There was only one Christian at Dunster House. We held the session in his room. Early on in this meeting, one student asked the question about what happens to the innocent man in Africa. I knew that either way I answered, I was in trouble. If I said, "Too bad, he's had it," everyone say, "Well, I'm not going to have anything to do with your Christianity," or "What kind of religion condemns an innocent man?" and they would all troop out of the room. On the other hand,

10. Of course, Christ died for intellectual doubters, too, but only because they are also sinners.
11. He was in fact giving the talks that were later turned into the book *Basic Christianity.*

if I said, "God is a gracious, loving God, and I'm sure He has provision for that innocent man," their answer would be, "Well, if those people are going to heaven without the gospel, a nice guy like me doesn't have anything to worry about."

I knew I had to avoid the question. I prayed, and my next thought seemed like an answer from the Lord. I asked the fellow this question: "Who is more important to you—you or this man in Africa?"

He said, "What do you mean?"

"Who's number one? Who do you feed first, you or the man in Africa? Who are you most concerned about?"

"Well," he said, "I guess I'm most concerned about me."

"Now let me answer the same question. Between you and the man in Africa, I'm more concerned about you. If I were more concerned about the man in Africa, I'd be in Africa. But since you are number one in your life, and you're number one in my life, let's talk about you, and after we finish with that, we'll talk about secondary things."

Well, everybody laughed, which embarrassed him, but at the same time everyone else at the meeting was suddenly on my side, which meant that he was not the leader of the pack anymore—I was. He was getting fed to the dogs instead of me.

To defend himself he said, "I don't think you know the answer."

I said, "Believe me, I *do* know the answer, and I'm not going to tell you."

He went to hear John Stott that evening. I don't know if he became a Christian, but I do know that we did not get into any senseless controversies.

When I was living in Yokosuka and working in the office of the Chief of Staff for Communication, there was a
brilliant lieutenant junior-grade working in the same communications facility. He was a graduate of a Jesuit institution
and an atheist. He was very egocentric—the kind of fellow
you did not dare beat playing ping-pong because he would
throw the paddle. His favorite word to describe everyone
was "stupid." The Admiral was "stupid," the Chief of Staff
was "stupid," everybody down the line was "stupid." He had
heard me comment positively about a certain commander
that he had put in his "stupid" book, so that made me "stupid," too. He did not know I was a Christian.

One night in the BOQ we were talking professional
subjects. I did not have the brains that this fellow had, but
I had more education and more experience in the field. I
had been communications officer on a destroyer for thirty
months during the Korean War, had a year of post-graduate
work in command communications, and at the time I was a
troubleshooter for Commander Naval Forces Far East. He
had only been in the Navy eighteen months. I was not trying
to "one-up" him, but as we talked it became apparent to him
that I knew more than he did.

At the end of the conversation, I realized that I had gotten
out of his "stupid" book and that he respected me for knowing more about the field than he did. As I got up to go to my
room, I turned and said, "Vic, the next time I talk to you, I'm
going to talk to you about God," and left. He could not fight
it—I had just gotten out of his "stupid" book! Of course, he
could have put me back in it really fast, but he did not dare
because he did not know what I was going to say about God.

I let him think about it for two days. Then I took my Bible,
knocked on his door, and went in. He was looking in the

mirror, tying his necktie. He looked like he was about to go out. I said, "Vic, I've come to talk to you about God. Unless you have other plans, I'll stay."

He said, "I had other plans, but I just changed them. Sit down." He went to his closet, pulled out a book, sat on his bunk, and opened the book. About two-thirds of the way through there was a paragraph underlined in red on the left-hand page. With this book open in front of him, he said, "Okay, shoot. Prove to me that there's a God."

"No, Vic, I didn't come to prove God; I came to declare Him."

"Unless you prove God, there's no basis for a conversation."

"Nevertheless, I'm not going to prove Him." I said, "Suppose there is a God, an omnipotent God, and He made billions of stars, billions of people, billions of buttercups, and billions of raindrops, and you stand up in front of this omnipotent God and say, 'Show me, God, and then I'll believe.' He doesn't have to show you—you are one of two billion! I'm His representative, I don't have to show you, and I'm not going to show you." He closed his book.

I assume that the paragraph underlined in red somehow wiped out God, and if I had gone ahead and "proved" Him, Vic would have used the paragraph, and we would have argued until two o'clock in the morning.

After Vic closed his book, he said, "Well, what are you going to talk about, then?"

"I thought I'd start with the subject of sin."

He yelled, "Sin?! There's no such thing as sin! Sin where?"

"Well, since you asked, it's the sin in Vic Jensen that I'm concerned about."

He laughed again—it was a hollow laugh this time—and said, "There's no sin in me!" But he knew that there was, and he knew that *I* knew there was.

I said to him, "Are you telling me that you have no conscience?" Have you ever felt guilty and known that everybody else knew it? I could see the guilt in his face as he reflected on his conscience, and he changed the subject.

"What are you going to use for an authority?"

I said, "Well, I brought my Bible; I thought I'd use that."

When I said I thought I would use my Bible for an authority, it was not that I had doubts about whether it was authoritative. It was a confident understatement, which is far more powerful than saying, "I BROUGHT MY BIBLE, THE INSPIRED WORD OF GOD, AND IT'S AN AUTHORITY!" *That* would make him wonder whether it really was. When you shout, it undermines your authority. Like the minister who put in his notes, "Argument weak, shout here," when you find yourself shouting, *know* that you have just told everyone listening that you are *unsure* of your beliefs. I said, "I brought my Bible; I thought I'd use that for an authority."

He knew that I knew it was authoritative. Again he objected strongly: "You can't use that for an authority!"

"Why not?"

"For two reasons. First, the Bible is not authorized in intercollegiate debate. Second, I will not accept it as an authority, and I don't believe it!"

"In the first place, this isn't intercollegiate debate. It's war, and the rules are different. In the second place, I don't *care* if you don't accept it as an authority. Of *course* you don't believe it; you haven't heard it!" (For the Bible says that faith comes by hearing and hearing by the Word of God.)

I said, "Suppose I had a broadsword in my hand and I said, 'Jensen, I'm going to chop off your head,' and you laugh at me and say, 'Wilson, you can't chop off my head, because I don't believe that's a sword.' Then it's *my* turn to laugh. Whether you *believe* it is a sword has nothing to do with it. If I sheath the sword and say, 'Well, he doesn't believe it's a sword, so I guess I can't chop off his head,' that only proves that *I* don't believe it's a sword! 'The Word of God is quick and powerful and sharper than any two-edged sword, dividing asunder between the soul and spirit, joints and marrow, discerning the thoughts and intents of the heart' (Hebrews 4:12). I'm going to have your head."[12]

I continued, "What do you think the Bible is? Fiction?"

"Yeah, fiction."

"You mean like *Pogo* or *Terry and the Pirates* in the funny papers?"

"About in that category."

"Do you read *Pogo*?"

"Oh, yeah, I love *Pogo*."

"*Terry and the Pirates*?"

"Yeah, I read fiction all the time."

"Then you won't mind if I read you a few chapters of fiction."

Why do people not want you to read the Word of God to them? Because they do not believe it? No—because they are afraid it might be true. I said, "If it's fiction, you won't mind

12. When I told Vic that I would have his head, it was not jesting. It was serious. Most jesting is deadly and quarrel-causing because it has a put-down quality to it. We might be tempted to think it is kinder to jest about some things, but in reality it just makes it more difficult. So I am generally dead serious in witnessing situations, especially when talking with people who have spent all their lives quarreling and arguing. They will respect directness even though they would rather have a quarrel.

at all," and I read him the first eight chapters of Romans. He sat and listened—no quarrels, no arguments. A few days later he came down to my room and said, "Let's have some more of the book." I read him the first five chapters of Acts. That time I gave him a Bible so he could follow along as I read out loud. Later I read him the next thirteen chapters of Acts, the resurrection account in the four gospels, and 1 Corinthians 15.

Shortly after that Vic received orders to the Atlantic fleet. Right before he left, I gave him a copy of Billy Graham's *Peace With God*. I gave it to him just as he was leaving so he would not pack it and ship it with the rest of his things. I do not know whether he ever became a Christian; that was the last time I saw him. But I know he got well plowed and super-planted, and I believe that he is a Christian today.

> But avoid foolish and ignorant disputes, knowing that they generate strife. And a servant of the Lord *must not quarrel* but be gentle to all, able to teach, patient, in humility correcting those who are in opposition, if God perhaps will grant them repentance, so that they may know the truth. (2 Tim. 2:23-25 NKJV)

When we are kind, gentle, and willing to teach, people receive it, often even those who look like they are itching for a fight from the first. Stay out of quarrels and teach those who oppose you kindly and gently. That does not mean avoiding the opposition. Just continue the encounter on *your* terms, not on theirs.

It *is* possible to hold the fort and be kind. The more intense you get, the more quarrelsome you get, and the more defensive people become—but you need to get them to drop their guard. You cannot break it down with strident answers, however true those answers might be.

CHAPTER 9

ASSURANCES OF SALVATION

Once someone has become a Christian, how can they know that they have?

> I write these things to you who believe in the name of the Son of God so that you may know that you have eternal life. (1 John 5:13)

I talk about the assurances of salvation for several reasons: 1) to help some people who think they are Christians find out that they are not, 2) to help people who are Christians know for certain that they are saved, and 3) to find out for myself if someone else is saved.

Some people are not real Christians but think they are. They usually come from nominal Christian backgrounds or second-generation-Christian families. It is difficult to present the gospel to someone who already believes he is a Christian. It is also not wise for you to *tell* these people they are not Christians, because they get defensive. But if you help them *find out for themselves* that they are not Christians, they may want to know how to become one. It is the same with people who think they are not Christians when they really *are*; you need to help them find that out for themselves, too.

Years ago in Annapolis, Maryland, a woman came into our bookstore. She was about to begin a class on the book of Acts for post-high school kids and wanted help. I gave her *Acts of the Apostles* by Campbell Morgan and shared a few thoughts on how to talk to that age group. The following Monday, she called up and said, "It worked, it worked, it worked! One of the girls was going to marry a Catholic boy, and she came to me after the class for counsel. It was wonderful. "

"What did you tell her?"

"I told her everything that was wrong with the Catholic Church."

"Was she receptive?"

"No," she said, "She didn't accept it very well at all."

"Well, the Catholic Church might not be the problem. The question is not whether the boy is a Catholic, but whether he is a Christian. Maybe *she* is not a Christian. Ask her if she is assured of her salvation. Then tell her that you are sure of *yours*. You are sure, aren't you?"

She said, "No, I'm not sure." I went through the assurances of salvation with her, and she realized that she was not a Christian. She got off the telephone and put her trust in the Savior. Later she went through the assurances with her 18-year-old daughter who immediately received Christ.

What are these assurances of salvation?

LOVING CHRISTIANS

> We know that we have passed from death to life, because
> we love our brothers. Anyone who does not love remains in
> death. (1 John 3:14)

Loving other Christians is evidence of your salvation.
In her autobiography, *Climbing*, Rosalind Goforth tells of
an older man who was unsure of his salvation. He said, "I
wanted to convince myself all these years that I'm going to
heaven, but I can't." She asked him if he loved the Lord's
people. He said, "Oh, it's my greatest joy in life to be with
the Lord's people on the Lord's day singing the Lord's prais-
es." She pointed him to 1 John 3:14: "We know that we have
passed from death to life because we love our brothers."

Suppose you brought a non-Christian to church. He
would not feel comfortable. He might admire and respect
Christians, but he wouldn't love them like they love each
other. He cannot. Pagans love pagans and Christians are to
love pagans; it takes a *Christian* to love a Christian.

When you love other Christians, you know that you are
saved, and everyone else knows, too:

> A new command I give you: Love one another. As I have
> loved you, so you must love one another. By this *all men* will
> know that you are My disciples, if you love one another.
> (John 13:34-35)

I once tried to set up two midshipmen with a couple of
girls, only to find out that one of the girls was engaged. I
had not known that, so the next time I saw her, I asked,
"Barbara, is this guy you are going to marry a Christian?"

"Oh, yes."

"How do you know?"

"Well, he goes to the same church I go to. He sings in the choir with me."

"How long have you gone to that church?"

"Years."

"How long have you been a Christian?"

"Three months."

I said, "What were you before then?"

"Just a church-goer."

"How do you know he's not just a church-goer?"

She said, "I'll send him right in."

Shortly afterward her fiancé came in. He was a rough fellow, and he did not look happy. I did not know what effect Barbara had had on him, but I assumed there had been some ground plowed. We sat down, and I gave him the gospel. I even gave an invitation for him to receive Christ, but he wasn't interested. He had done his duty, I had done mine, and off he went.

Shortly before Christmas, I ran into him on the street. He looked at me and said, "Boy, am I glad to see you!" then walked back to the store with me. It turned out that he had been singing in the choir at the Methodist church, and halfway through a hymn he had believed and been converted. He began to sing like he had never sung before, so heartily that the choir director and other choir members said, "Larry, what happened to you?"

This Larry was first trumpet in the Naval Academy band. One of the band members, a clarinet player, was also the pastor of the Church of Christ in Annapolis. The Church of Christ claims that it is not just a denomination, but *the* church of Christ. As other band members were converted through Larry, the clarinet-playing pastor would try to get them to join the Church of Christ.

I had several conversations with this pastor. He did not think that I was a Christian or that the new converts from the band were, either. One time I invited him to a Christian concert near the bookstore. Afterward, we went to my office and talked. I said, "The reason I called you in is to tell you I do not think you are a Christian."

He looked at me in shock. Nobody had ever said that to him before. He was a *pastor*. He asked me why I thought he was not a Christian.

"Because of 1 John 3:14: 'We know that we have passed from death to life because we love our brothers.' Loving the brethren is not the *means* of passing from death to life. It is the means of knowing that you *have* passed from death to life. I see it in me; I see it in others. But you don't love any of them!

"Also in John 13: 34 and 35, 'A new command I give you: Love one another…By this all men will know that you are My disciples, if you love one another.' Love for the brethren is a means of the whole world knowing you're saved. I don't see you loving any of the brothers, so I have every good, biblical reason to suspect that you are not a Christian.

"I know that you do not believe in playing instrumental music in a worship service.[13] As far as I'm concerned, you can sing *a capella* to the Lord, and the Lord will receive it just as well. That's not a problem. The problem is that you condemn people who sing some other way. What's more, you refuse to play the piano or any musical instrument for the glory of the Lord, but you play the clarinet for the Devil all week in the Naval Academy band!"

13. The Church of Christ is against using instrumental music in church.

That really shook him up. It unnerved him so much that he wrote a letter to the Department of the Navy as a conscientious objector, not for shooting people, but for playing the clarinet. Several years later he phoned me to say he had been converted in Toronto and was attending a charismatic Presbyterian church in Dallas. Our conversation had helped him to realize that he was not a Christian.

OBEDIENCE

We know that we have come to know Him if we obey His commands. (1 John 2:3)

Keeping God's commandments is not the means of knowing Him. That would be works-righteousness. Rather, your increased ability to obey the commandments of the Lord after you are converted is evidence that you *already know* Him. The King James translation says, "Hereby we do *know* that we know Him, if we keep His commandments."

The man who says, "I know Him," but does not do what He commands is a liar, and the truth is not in him. But if anyone obeys His word, God's love is truly made complete in him. This is how we know we are in Him: Whoever claims to live in Him must walk as Jesus did. (1 John 2:4-6)

No one who lives in Him keeps on sinning. No one who continues to sin has either seen Him or known Him. (1 John 3:6)

No one who is born of God will continue to sin, because God's seed remains in him; he cannot go on sinning, because he has been born of God. This is how we know who the children of God are and who the children of the devil are:

Anyone who does not do what is right is not a child of God, nor is anyone who does not love his brother. (1 John 3:9-1)

We know that anyone born of God does not continue to sin; the one who was born of God keeps him safe, and the evil one cannot harm him. (1 John 5:18)

When we are no longer living in sin, we know we are saved. If it looks like we are living in sin, there is no reason for others to think that we are Christians, and no reason for us to, either.

DISCIPLINE

If obedience is a means of knowing that you know the Lord, what happens when you disobey?

I tell you the truth, whoever hears My word and believes Him who sent Me has eternal life and will not be condemned; he has crossed over from death to life. (John 5:24)

If I hear and believe right now, I have eternal life *now*. By definition, eternal is eternal. I cannot lose it. It is not "eternal until I sin tomorrow." If obedience after conversion is evidence of salvation, then when we disobey, if we have eternal life, that disobedience brings with it the next assurance of salvation:

And you have forgotten that word of encouragement that addresses you as sons: "My son, do not make light of the Lord's discipline, and do not lose heart when He rebukes you, because the Lord disciplines those He loves, and He punishes everyone He accepts as a son." Endure hardship as discipline; God is treating you as sons. For what son is not disciplined by his father? *If you are not disciplined* (and everyone undergoes discipline), *then you are illegitimate children and not true sons.* Moreover, we have all had human fathers who disciplined us and we respected them for it. How much more should we submit to the Father of our spirits and live! Our fathers disciplined us for a little while as they thought best; but God disciplines us for our good, that we may share in His holiness. No discipline seems pleasant at the time, but painful. Later on, however, it produces a harvest of righteousness and peace for those who have been trained by it. (Heb. 12:5-11)

If you are not disciplined, you are not a true son. God does not discipline those who are not His children. If you are getting away with your disobedience, you are not a child of God. If you are being disciplined, pay attention and repent: it is evidence that you are saved.

In one sense, people are bothered by their conscience before they are converted, but not like they are afterwards. Before conversion, you can commit many little sins and never be bothered, but when you do them after conversion, you get convicted. Meanwhile, people around you are getting away with terrible sins, apparently feeling *nothing.* That says they are not sons.

When a Christian is disciplined, he loses his joy in the Lord. Should you despair at this? Are you not a Christian because you don't have any joy? No! On the contrary—that loss of joy is evidence that you *are* a Christian.

A girl came into the bookstore one day and said, "Mr. Wilson, I want to become a Christian." Her ground had been plowed, but I did not know if she was ready to be harvested. I talked about the gospel to find out. She told me she believed that Jesus Christ is the Son of God, that He died for her, was buried, and rose again for her. I said, "You know the gospel, and you have understanding and a desire. There's only one thing left, and that's the decision."

She said, "Yeah, I know. But I just can't do it."

I didn't know what the problem was, so I decided to probe a little bit.

"Tell me, do you love sin?"

She thought for a minute and said, "I *hate* it."

I thought to myself, "Well, I don't know what her inhibition is, but I am going to increase her desire for the kingdom so much that the desire will overcome the inhibition."

I started with this:

> The man without the Spirit does not accept the things that come from the Spirit of God, for they are foolishness to him, and he cannot understand them, because they are spiritually discerned. (1 Cor. 2:14)

The man without the Spirit cannot understand the things that come from the Spirit of God. When a person becomes a Christian, the Bible, which is spiritual truth, suddenly turns into English. I told this to the girl.

She said, "The Bible already makes sense to me." She said it in a very sure way, in such a way I knew that she was already a Christian.

"How long has it made sense to you?"

"Three weeks." She had just told me when she'd become a Christian. I thought, "This is wonderful. I know she's a Christian, and she doesn't!"

"Tell me: before three weeks ago, did you love Christians?"

She said, "I didn't know any."

"Tell me about your brother-in-law. What did you think of him before three weeks ago?"[14]

---

14. I did not ask about her sister, because that would be a sister-love.

"I couldn't stand him."

"What's he been like in the last three weeks?"

"Oh," she said, "he's become a really great guy."

"Before three weeks ago, had you ever done anything really bad?"

"Yes, I did."

"Did it bother your conscience then?"

"Yes, all the time."

"Think about that thing right now. Do the bad things you did a month ago bother your conscience right now?"

She thought for a minute and said, "No." They had been forgiven three weeks earlier.

"How about the little things that you do every day? Did they bother you before three weeks ago?"

"No, they didn't."

"How do you feel about them right now?"

"They're killing me!"

"That's funny. Are you telling me that the great big thing you did before doesn't bother you, but now all these little things do bother you?"

"That's right."

"What did you do three weeks ago?"

"What do you mean?"

"Did you pray?"

"Yes, I prayed."

"What did you pray?"

"I didn't know how to pray. I just made up my own prayer."

"That's alright. Would you tell me what you prayed?"

"Well, I just told the Lord Jesus He could do whatever He wanted with me."

I said, "I think He's done it." I pointed out that the things she had experienced were evidence that she had passed from death to life three weeks earlier. The reason she had come in to the bookstore to become a Christian was that her conscience was *killing* her. She thought she could not possibly be a Christian because she was convicted of the little sins she had committed over the previous three weeks. She did not have any joy, but it was only the discipline of the Lord on His child.

THE HOLY SPIRIT

We know that we live in Him and He in us, because He has given us of His Spirit. (1 John 4:13)

Those who are led by the Spirit of God are sons of God. (Rom. 8:14)

This verse does not say that being led by the Spirit of God makes you a son of God; it tells you who the sons of God are —"those who are led by the Spirit of God."

The Spirit Himself testifies with our spirit that we are God's children. Now if we are children, then we are heirs—heirs of God and co-heirs with Christ, if indeed we share in His sufferings in order that we may also share in His glory. (Rom. 8:16-17)

Sons and heirs. Heirs of God and joint heirs with Christ. God's Spirit talks to our spirit to tell us that we belong to Him. We are His children. I cannot explain it, but to those to whom this has happened it does not need explaining.

The Spirit is an indwelling witness:

And this is His command: to believe in the name of His Son, Jesus Christ, and to love one another as He commanded us. Those who obey His commands live in Him, and He in them. And this is how we know that He lives in us: *We know it by the Spirit He gave us.* (1 John 3:23-24)

The Holy Spirit is a guarantee of our final salvation, the resurrection of our bodies:

And you also were included in Christ when you heard the word of truth, the gospel of your salvation. Having believed, you were marked in Him with a seal, *the promised Holy Spirit,* who is *a deposit guaranteeing our inheritance* until the redemption of those who are God's possession—to the praise of his glory. (Eph. 1:13-14)

Now it is God who has made us for this very purpose and *has given us the Spirit as a deposit,* guaranteeing what is to come. (2 Cor. 5:5)

Whoever does not have the Spirit does not belong to Christ. He is not a Christian. He is not saved:

You, however, are controlled not by the sinful nature but by the Spirit, if the Spirit of God lives in you. And *if anyone does not have the Spirit of Christ, he does not belong to Christ.* (Rom. 8:9)

Those who are sons of God are led by the Spirit:

Those who are led by the Spirit of God are sons of God. (Rom. 8:14)

But if you are led by the Spirit, you are not under law. (Gal. 5:18)

A midshipman in the class of '61 came to the Christian meetings at the Naval Academy for a while. He looked miserable all the time. Bible study made him miserable, prayer made him miserable, singing hymns made him miserable. Finally I had a talk with him about the gospel. The following fall he was back at the Christian meetings, singing hymns with great joy and loving the Bible study.

"What happened?" I asked him. "Last spring you were unhappy singing hymns, unhappy in the presence of believers, and unhappy with the Word of God. How could these three things make you miserable last year, but happy this year?"

He said, "Remember that commitment you talked about? I made it right after we parted that day."

"Well, if you did, you ought to have some evidence besides what I've seen. Tell me, have you seen the Holy Spirit guide you?"

"Yes. I had orders for the summer to a destroyer out of Norfolk, Virginia. Right after I made that decision, my orders were changed to a submarine out of Charleston. I got off in Guantanamo Bay to go to chapel on the base, thinking I was the only one going, when a lieutenant came off the submarine. He was going to chapel, too, so we went together. We spent the whole cruise in the book of Romans."

The lieutenant he had mentioned was one of the godliest men in the Atlantic fleet. The Holy Spirit led this midshipman to where he would get established in the faith, because those who are sons of God are led by the Spirit of God.

If you have not been led by the Spirit, or if you have and do not recognize it, you should wonder if you are saved.

For who among men knows the thoughts of a man except the man's spirit within him? In the same way no one knows the thoughts of God except the Spirit of God. We have not received the spirit of the world but the Spirit who is from God, that we may understand what God has freely given us. This is what we speak, not in words taught us by human wisdom but in words taught by the Spirit, expressing spiritual truths in spiritual words. *The man without the Spirit does not accept the things that come from the Spirit of God, for they are foolishness to him, and he cannot understand them, because they are spiritually discerned.* The spiritual man makes judgments about all things, but he himself is not subject to any man's judgment: "For who has known the mind of the Lord that he may instruct Him?" But we have the mind of Christ. (1 Cor. 2:11-16)

The natural man may be well-educated and a genius, but unless he has the Spirit of God, the Word of God is foolishness to him.

CHANGE OF CHARACTER

The acts of the sinful nature are obvious: sexual immorality, impurity and debauchery; idolatry and witchcraft; hatred, discord, jealousy, fits of rage, selfish ambition, dissensions, factions and envy; drunkenness, orgies, and the like. I warn you, as I did before, that those who live like this will not inherit the kingdom of God. (Gal. 5:19-21)

If this describes your normal state, you will not inherit the kingdom of God.

But the fruit of the Spirit is love, joy, peace, patience, kindness, goodness, faithfulness, gentleness and self-control. Against such things there is no law. (Gal. 5:22-23)

If this describes you, you are saved. If you find yourself in both lists, it is for one of the following reasons:

1. You are mistaking natural personality traits for part of the fruit of the Spirit. They are not. The fruit of the

Spirit is the characteristics of God given to a person when he is saved.

2. You are saved but are deliberately choosing to go back into the first list. Confess and forsake it right now.

3. You are naturally in the first list, but faking the second list. That is, you are a hypocrite. You are not saved.

Many years ago, when Bessie was still holding regular women's Bible studies, there were three sisters in her study. Two of them were clearly Christians. The third was a member of one of the strongest gospel churches in the city, and she knew all the answers in the Bible study, but she was an alcoholic and a drug addict. Bessie was convinced she was not a Christian, but the woman would not listen. She "knew" when she had received Christ. One day she telephoned, and I talked with her.

"Would you mind if I read you a verse of Scripture?" I asked.

She said no. I read her the first passage from Galatians 5.

"Tell me, have you ever been guilty of any of those?"

"About half of them."

"Let me read you the next verse. 'But the fruit of the Spirit is love, joy, peace, patience, kindness, goodness, faithfulness, gentleness and self-control. Against such things there is no law.' How about these?"

"None of those!" She had all the right doctrine, but half of the works of the flesh and *none* of the fruit of the Spirit. She said, "I see I'm not a Christian." It was not much later that she put her trust in Christ.

The Bible describes what happens to a person at conversion, even if he does not *know* it has happened:

Therefore, if anyone is in Christ, he is a new creation; the old has gone, the new has come! (2 Cor. 5:17).

The new Christian has *already* experienced this. The Holy Spirit has done the work in you.

CONFESSING JESUS AS LORD

Therefore I tell you that no one who is speaking by the Spirit of God says, "Jesus be cursed," and no one can say, "Jesus is Lord," except by the Holy Spirit. (1 Cor. 12:3)

If you confess with your mouth, "Jesus is Lord," and believe in your heart that God raised Him from the dead, you will be saved. For it is with your heart that you believe and are justified, and it is with your mouth that you confess and are saved. (Rom. 10:9-10)

This confession is not a matter of the mouth only. People who are not saved say this in liturgies all of the time.

In Annapolis a Lutheran Church member came to see me at a friend's suggestion because her eighteen-year-old son was breaking into houses. She told me she could not understand it: he had grown up in the church, he was president of the youth group, and here he was, in trouble with the law. The more she talked, the more I realized that she was the problem. Finally I asked her what her position was doctrinally: I asked her if she believed in the deity of Jesus Christ, His death for our sins, and His resurrection from the dead. She replied that she did, and she believed that a person is justified by faith alone. She had all the right answers.

"If you died right now, where would you go?" I asked.

"I think I'd go to heaven."

"Why?"

"Because I sing in the choir and I never miss church." She had just told me that the way of salvation was by faith, and then she gave a completely different reason for her going to heaven.

It is possible to be brainwashed with the Scriptures. People give all the right answers, but they put their trust in something else. The United States is full of men and women who believe the gospel *academically*.

One of the students at the Lutheran college in Ann Arbor, Michigan, was a terrible complainer. I decided I was going to love him, so I listened to all his complaints. One day we began to talk, and I found out that he had not been to chapel at all since he came to the college. They had daily chapel, and though it was not required, there was strong pressure to go. I asked him why he had never gone.

"I think it's phony," he said.

I asked him why.

"I think there ought to be one big church, not just Lutherans, or Baptists, or Presbyterians."

"Boy, that sounds like a *wonderful* idea. But suppose the people who are pushing for one big church don't believe that Jesus Christ is the Son of God?"

"Oh," he said, "well, then they're not even Christians."

"Suppose they don't believe that He's risen from the dead?"

"Well, then they're not Christians."

I said, "Will you tell me where you stand on these things?"

"Certainly. I believe in the deity of Jesus Christ, His death for our sins, His resurrection from the dead. I believe in the virgin birth, and that you are saved by faith alone." He "four-pointed" his catechism.

"What would happen if you died right now? Where would you go?"

He said, "I haven't the faintest idea."

"Why don't you know?"

"I don't know how good you have to be to go to heaven."
He had the right answers, but he *trusted* in being good, and
he was not good.

In the first case, I pointed out to the Lutheran woman
how she had contradicted herself, and she went home and
became a Christian. I did the same thing to this boy, and he
went back to his room and became a Christian. He realized
that he had been putting his trust in something other than
what he *said* he was putting it in. When you hear people tell
you all the truth of the gospel, it does not necessarily mean
that is what they are *trusting*. It may just be what they have
learned to say by growing up in the church. Many orthodox
churches teach gospel so that it gets into people's heads only.
They end up putting their faith in works, just like any other
unsaved man.

One of the reasons there are so many false conversions in
churches is that kids are sent to Sunday school or confirmation class, and when they are twelve, they are baptized or
confirmed and join the church. Of course they answer the
questions properly, so their conversion is assumed, but the
evidence is not there. This is a great hindrance to real conversion.

I assume that people are not Christians until I see otherwise. I do not think it is wrong to do this. The Scripture
says, "Judge not, lest you be so judged" (Matthew 7:1), but
the sense of the text is really, "*Condemn* not, lest you be so
condemned." In light of this, I think it is wise to judge everyone I meet as not a Christian. In the first place, I am right
more often than not. In the second place, if I judge people
as Christians and therefore do not tell them the gospel, and
it turns out that they were not Christians, then I really have
"judged" them! On the other hand, when I judge them not

a Christian and proceed to tell them the good news, if it turns out that they were Christians the whole time, it does not hurt them a bit. We end up in fellowship.

When I was on the aircraft carrier *Hancock* in the East China Sea, I met with a small group of Christians to go to a chaplains' function. We saw a lieutenant there with a *Halley's Bible Handbook* in one hand and a big, black Bible in the other. We thought that he must be a Christian. We introduced ourselves and invited him to the evening Bible study in my room.

That night we happened to be in the third chapter of John. The lieutenant really got into the study. He shouted, "You must be born again!" We thought we had found a really "going" Christian. Then towards the end of study, I thought to myself, "Wait a minute! You've just judged this man a Christian; you've violated all your principles of evangelism!" I felt guilty for having judged him a Christian.

As soon as the study was over, I asked him about assurance of salvation, and he said, "Salvation, what's that?" He did not know anything about *anything*. We went through the gospel together. It was brand-new to him, and he called upon the Lord. After it was all over, I said, "Now, please tell me, what were you doing walking around with a Bible and a *Halley's Bible Handbook*?"

"Oh," he said, "I was looking for answers."

"How come you came out so strong on 'you must be born again' in the Bible study?"

"Well, that's what it said." He had not known anything.

Another time there was a woman who had gone to all the pastors in town for counseling. She had read nearly every Christian book out there but did not seem to have applied any of it. One day she knocked on our front door. Bessie sent her to the backyard to wait for me on the chairs under the apple tree.

I had been reading a book by Watchman Nee. It stated that two people can hear the same verse preached ("I am the way, the truth and the life, no man comes unto the Father but by Me" John 4:16), and one person says, "That's wonderful," and comes to the Father by Jesus Christ, while another person says, "That's wonderful—I'm going to make a plaque and put it on the wall."

I went to the backyard where she was waiting, and I told her what I had just read.

She said, "What's the difference between these two people? They both agreed with the text."

I said, "Well, the one fellow has love, joy, and peace, and the other fellow has a plaque on the wall. One person came to the Father, and one person came to the verse."

This hit her hard. She had come to all the verses. She called me the next day. "I'm not a Christian."

I said, "I didn't think so."

This woman had been arguing theology for years. It was hard to differ with her, because she would spout the same things I had told her. So I said to her, "I'm not going to tell you how to become a Christian. You'll just plug the formula again, it will not be any different than the last time. When you have some view of the holiness of God, and some view of how sinful you are in the light of His holiness, and then some view of the love of God in the light of your great sin and His holiness, then I will tell you how to become a Christian."

For a long time I did not hear from her. Then one day she called and asked, "How could the Father love the Son and send Him to the cross?" I knew right away she was beginning to understand.

I said, "Well, if you look at the text closely, it says 'for God so loved the *world*' (John 3:16). That tells us how much He loved the world—so much that He gave His only begotten Son."

I wanted to tell her about the love of God, but I decided not to tell her in prose because she ran everything through her head instead of her heart. So I told her everything in poetry. I recited the hymn "The Love of God" over the telephone, and I sang "The Deep, Deep Love of Jesus." I only spoke to her in ways that bypassed her brain and went straight to her heart. One day she was vacuuming the house and singing the chorus, "He is Lord, He is Lord, He has risen from the dead, and He is Lord," and she was converted in the middle of singing "He is Lord." She has walked with the Lord ever since.

Each one of these assurances, by itself, is not an absolute means of knowing you are saved. But the combination of them can reveal whether someone is a Christian or not. There may be exceptions, but if a church member has not really passed from death to life, he will come up with negative answers on some of these assurances. No, he does not love those pious people. No, he does not hurt when he does something wrong. No, the Bible does not make sense to him. As you share these Scriptures, he will be telling you and *himself* that he is not a Christian.

1 John was written "so that you may know that you have eternal life" (1 John 5:13). Do you want to know? Read the letter through several times. The third time, mark every occurrence of the word "know." Each verse will tell you how you can know that you have eternal life.

CHAPTER 10

Training and Teaching

TEACHING EVANGELISM

Giving advice on evangelism is an excellent opportunity for evangelism. Years ago I gave an eager 19-year-old "Christian" a book to help him evangelize others. Several years later I found out that he dated his conversion to Christ from the time he was halfway through the book.

Here are a few situations which might indicate such a need:

- Someone comes to you for advice on how to help a friend who is in serious trouble (pregnancy, stealing, or drugs).
- Someone comes wanting answers to "intellectual" questions in order to pass them on to a friend.
- A friend is looking for the right denomination to join, and he wants information to convince him to be a member of his own church.

These situations and ones like them cover hundreds of real cases. You should be alert to the possibility that the people coming to you may not be Christians.

Regardless of the spiritual state of the questioner, it is always a good idea to start out with the assurances of salvation. If he is a Christian who has had doubts about his own salvation, he will gain assurance of his relationship with the Lord. If he is a Christian and is sure of it, he will gain a more complete understanding of what he is offering to others in the gospel of Christ. If he is not a Christian, it may become apparent to him and perhaps also to you.

Here are a few pointers for talking to Christians about witnessing:

1. First, increase their confidence by recognition of what the Christian has in Christ: everlasting life, forgiveness of sins, power over temptation, freedom from fear of death, peace, joy, love, and communication with God.

2. Show the Christian that the non-Christian does not have these characteristics, no matter how confident he may appear on the outside. In fact, he has the opposite characteristics: he is afraid to die, he has a guilty conscience, and he cannot keep from sinning.

3. Teach them to obey 2 Timothy 2:24-26:

And a servant of the Lord *must not quarrel* but be gentle to all, able to teach, patient, in humility correcting those who are in opposition, if God perhaps will grant them repentance, so that they may know the truth, and that they may come to their senses and escape the snare of the devil, having been taken captive by him to do his will. (NKJV)

Winning arguments is not the same as winning people to Christ. Even mature Christians have to be careful not to overwhelm others with facts, arguments, and reasoning.

4. Teach the Christians to love and befriend someone they do not like. This may require some heart searching and recognition of prejudices. They must be willing to pray for the love of Christ for that person.

5. Encourage them to write a brief autobiography (600-1000 words) and include their own conversion in it. They do not have to memorize it, but writing it down will ensure that they have thought it through.

6. Help them understand the content of the gospel (see 1 Cor. 15:1-8). Look at where people were converted in the book of Acts and go over specifically what gospel content was used in each case.

7. Send them out, armed with prayer, to share what Christ means to them. Better yet, go out with them to the people they are concerned about.

INTERVENING

I have been asked what to do when you come upon a situation where a Christian is witnessing to an unbeliever and is just blowing it.

Do not stop him, and do not get upset. I have been in this kind of situation fairly regularly. Just let it go. Fighting or disagreeing with a fellow Christian in front of an unbeliever is much worse. If the other Christian is open to it, I might talk to him privately and tell him he hurt the witness, but if not, I usually don't say anything at all.

If you come across a Christian talking to a non-Christian, can you interject things? I used to do this, thinking that I could probably witness better than the other Christian, even if I did not think he was going about it in the wrong way. I do not do it anymore. Instead, I pray and trust that God will guide the other Christian. God has the floor; He knows what He is doing, and He has brought this person to do the witnessing. However, sometimes I wait around a moment to see if they will ask me to join the conversation. If they ask, then I come in; if they do not ask, I trust that God is working in it, and that maybe I would have been a competitive or conflicting witness.

Another sticky area is small group Bible studies with non-Christians attending. There always seems to be someone who is eager to get the gospel in. For instance, we might be studying in Philippians 4 (a passage not directly related to salvation), and all of a sudden someone says to me, "Jim, what does it mean to be born again?" The Christian is so afraid that the non-Christians will not get the gospel that he throws the ball to me, expecting me to expound on the new birth. I deliberately drop the ball every time.

If you are going to teach or witness along with another Christian, it is good to pray, talk, and study the Word together first. It is also good to get to know each other before you go to teach or witness. The aim is not to think, talk, and act like carbon copies of each other, but to be able to trust and understand each other. When the other person is talking, you should think, "I don't know where he's going, but I trust that God knows and that God is leading him in his conversation, so I'll pray for him." When you talk, it will not be contradictory to what your partner said, but complementary. If you do not trust him during teaching or witnessing, do not show it there. Trust that God will use it.

Often people come to me by reference from other Christians, and that can be either good or bad. I am glad, because it is an endorsement that God is using me. On the other hand, I am not glad to get people that others could have led to the Lord themselves. There is no sense in sending people to someone else when God wants to use *you*.

Many people want help for their problems. If they come to you and are given true wisdom that they see cannot possibly be just from you, they will come again and bring their friends. It is a humbling experience because you know that you really are a spokesman from God, not just through the Scriptures, but through the guidance of the Holy Spirit in your life. Trust God to use you that way. You do not need a special gift. God uses the people who *want* to be used. He will not send you someone He does not think you can handle. Look to the Word of God, your personal witness, and the guidance of the Holy Spirit.

TRAINING IN HOLINESS

We do not send infants into war. However, Christians enter the spiritual war as soon as they are born again and are very effective as evangelists in those first weeks. I know one Christian who led several of his friends to Christ in the week following his conversion. A decade later, he came to me after spending four years in seminary and asked me how to lead someone to Christ.

It is not necessary to train Christians in evangelism. It *is* necessary to train them in holiness.

In fact, though by this time you ought to be teachers, you
need someone to teach you the elementary truths of God's
word all over again. You need milk, not solid food! Anyone
who lives on milk, being still an infant, is not acquainted
with the teaching about righteousness. But solid food is for
the mature, who by constant use have trained themselves to
distinguish good from evil. (Heb. 5:12-14)

Brothers, I could not address you as spiritual but as worldly—mere infants in Christ. I gave you milk, not solid food,
for you were not yet ready for it. Indeed, you are still not
ready. You are still worldly. For since there is jealousy and
quarreling among you, are you not worldly? Are you not acting like mere men? (1 Cor. 3:1-3)

Holy, godly Christians are effective evangelists even if
they have not been trained in the methods of evangelism.

TEACHING AS A GIFT

And when he found him, he brought him to Antioch. So
for a whole year Barnabas and Saul met with the church and
taught great numbers of people. The disciples were called
Christians first at Antioch. (Acts 11:26)

Now you are the body of Christ, and each one of you is a
part of it. And in the church God has appointed first of all
apostles, second prophets, third teachers, then workers of
miracles, also those having gifts of healing, those able to help
others, those with gifts of administration, and those speaking in different kinds of tongues. Are all apostles? Are all
prophets? Are all teachers? Do all work miracles? Do all have
gifts of healing? Do all speak in tongues? Do all interpret?

But eagerly desire the greater gifts. And now I will show you the most excellent way. (1 Cor. 12:27-31)

This list is in order of importance: "First of all apostles, second prophets, *third teachers.*" Are all teachers? That is a rhetorical question. The answer is no. But we are told to "*eagerly desire* the greater gifts." Being a teacher is one of these.

Over the years I have known many people who desired to be in full-time Christian service. Very few have wanted to be in evangelism. They say they do not have the *gift* of evangelism. They want to be teachers or disciplers. However, they do not say they have the *gift* of being a teacher. They intend to be trained in how to teach instead. They are sidestepping the desire for the gift and replacing it with training.

It is amazing that we think evangelism requires a gift but teaching requires only training. Ungifted teachers are a great problem in the church today.

> *Not many of you should presume to be teachers*, my brothers, because you know that we who teach will be judged more strictly. (Jas. 3:1)

"Eagerly desire the greater gifts." "Not many of you should presume to be teachers." Contradiction? No. One is a desire for a gift from God. The other is presumption.

WHEN THE GOSPEL IS INEFFECTIVE

Here is a quotation from *The Soul Winner's Secret* by Colonel S.L. Brengle of the Salvation Army, 1918:

> That a man by personal magnetism, grace of manners, power or persuasiveness of speech, and a certain skill in playing upon the emotions and self-interest of the people, [can] create an excitement that fairly simulates a revival, and yet have

divided heart, I admit; but that he can bring men to a thorough repentance and renunciation of sin, a hearty embrace of the cross, an affectionate surrender to Jesus as a personal savior and Master who requires deep humility and meekness and tender love as the marks of His disciples is hard to be proved.[15]

Perhaps the gospel is ineffective because we have trained eloquent evangelists who by their charisma and persuasiveness succeed in getting many people to apparently respond to the gospel. These evangelists are trained, but not Holy Spirit-filled, and the "converts" are not born again of the Spirit, but only caught up in the emotion of the meeting. Although some people have passed from death into life through these glib evangelists with their truncated presentations of the gospel, the percentage is not a high one.

15. S. L. Brengle, *The Soul Winner's Secret* (London: Salvationist Publishing & Supplies Ltd., 1960).

CHAPTER 11

CONCLUSION

This book was written to encourage all of the saints to be aware that they are already witnesses for Jesus Christ. They may be good witnesses or bad witnesses, but they *are* witnesses.

> That which was from the beginning, which we have heard, which we have seen with our eyes, which we have looked at and our hands have touched—this we proclaim concerning the Word of life. The life appeared; we have seen it and testify to it, and we proclaim to you the eternal life, which was with the Father and has appeared to us. We proclaim to you what we have seen and heard, so that you also may have fellowship with us. And our fellowship is with the Father and with his Son, Jesus Christ. (1 John 1:1-3)

Here is how to be a good witness for Christ in your day-to-day life:

1. Walk in the light:

This is the message we have heard from him and declare to you: God is light; in him there is no darkness at all...But if we walk in the light, as he is in the light, we have fellowship with one another, and the blood of Jesus, his Son, purifies us from all sin...If we confess our sins, he is faithful and just and will forgive us our sins and purify us from all unrighteousness. (1 John 1:5, 7, 9)

2. Love God:

Jesus replied: "Love the Lord your God with all your heart and with all your soul and with all your mind." (Matt. 22:37)

3. Love your neighbor:

And the second is like it: "Love your neighbor as yourself." (Matt. 22:39)

4. Love your brother:

A new command I give you: Love one another. As I have loved you, so you must love one another. By this all men will know that you are my disciples, if you love one another. (John 13:34-35)

5. Love your enemy:

But I tell you who hear me: Love your enemies, do good to those who hate you, bless those who curse you, pray for those who mistreat you. If someone strikes you on one cheek, turn to him the other also. If someone takes your cloak, do not stop him from taking your tunic. Give to everyone who asks you, and if anyone takes what belongs to you, do not demand it back. Do to others as you would have them do to you. If you love those who love you, what credit is that to you? Even "sinners" love those who love them. And if you do good to those who are good to you, what credit is that to you? Even "sinners" do that. And if you lend to those from whom you expect repayment, what credit is that to you? Even "sinners" lend to "sinners," expecting to be repaid in full. But love your enemies, do good to them, and lend to them without expecting to get anything back. Then your reward will be great, and you will be sons of the Most High, because he is kind to the ungrateful and wicked. Be merciful, just as your Father is merciful. (Luke 6:27-36)

6. Love your wife:

Husbands, love your wives, just as Christ loved the church and gave himself up for her to make her holy, cleansing her by the washing with water through the word, and to present her to himself as a radiant church, without stain or wrinkle or any other blemish, but holy and blameless. (Eph. 5:25-27)

7. Pray for harvesters:

Then he said to his disciples, "The harvest is plentiful but the workers are few. Ask the Lord of the harvest, therefore, to send out workers into his harvest field." (Matt. 9:37-38)

8. Be alert to the spiritual state of everyone you meet.
9. Believe that there is a ripe harvest:

Do you not say, "Four months more and then the harvest"? I tell you, open your eyes and look at the fields! They are ripe for harvest. Even now the reaper draws his wages, even now he harvests the crop for eternal life, so that the sower and the reaper may be glad together. Thus the saying "One sows and another reaps" is true. I sent you to reap what you have not worked for. Others have done the hard work, and you have reaped the benefits of their labor. (John 4:35-38)

10. Believe 1 Timothy 2:3-6:

This is good, and pleases *God our Savior*, who *wants all men to be saved* and to come to a knowledge of the truth. For there is one God and one mediator between God and men, the man Christ Jesus, who gave himself as a ransom for all men—the testimony given in its proper time.

11. Know the gospel:

Now, brothers, I want to remind you of the gospel I preached to you, which you received and on which you have taken your stand. By this gospel you are saved, if you hold firmly to the word I preached to you. Otherwise, you have believed in vain. For what I received I passed on to you as of first importance: that Christ died for our sins according to the Scriptures, that he was buried, that he was raised on the third day according to the Scriptures, and that he appeared to Peter, and then to the Twelve. (1 Cor. 15:1-5)

12. Ask God to lead you to people who are in great spiritual need (see Acts 8, 9, and 10).

13. Believe Acts 4:12:

Salvation is found in no one else, for there is no other name under heaven given to men by which we must be saved. (Acts 4:12)

14. Believe Ezekiel 33:7-9:

Son of man, I have made you a watchman for the house of Israel; so hear the word I speak and give them warning from me. When I say to the wicked, "O wicked man, you will surely die," and you do not speak out to dissuade him from his ways, that wicked man will die for his sin, and I will hold you accountable for his blood. But if you do warn the wicked man to turn from his ways and he does not do so, he will die for his sin, but you will have saved yourself.

15. Believe Matthew 28:18-20:

Then Jesus came to them and said, "All authority in heaven and on earth has been given to me. Therefore go and make disciples of all nations, baptizing them in the name of the Father and of the Son and of the Holy Spirit, and teaching them to obey everything I have commanded you. And surely I am with you always, to the very end of the age."

For further study on walking in the light read:

The Calvary Road by Roy Hession
Continuous Revival by Norman Grubb
How to be Free From Bitterness by Jim Wilson
How to Maintain Joy in Your Life by Jim Wilson
Repentance and Restitution by Jim Wilson

Read through the conversations Jesus had with unbelievers. Read 1 Corinthians 1:18-2:5 and 1 Thessalonians 1:4-2:13. Read the companion books to this one: *Principles of War* and *Weapons & Tactics*.

What you learn, obey, imitate, and apply.